Heartbreak

Doesn't

Last Forever

N. Lee

ISBN-13: 9789188459008

Distributed by:

Emerentsia Publications
Marielundsvägen 9c
711 95 Gusselby
Sweden
emerentsiabooks.com

Published under the non-fiction imprint **Oh! With Dots**, an imprint owned by Emerentsia Publications.

Ordering Information:

Orders by U.S. trade bookstores and wholesalers. Please contact Ingram: One Ingram Blvd., La Vergne, TN 37086 • 615.793.5000 or visit www.ingramcontent.com.

Independently printed as a Swedish publication.

Interior design and layout by Emerentsia Publications.

3

The information given in this book is not meant as legal advice, medical or mental health advice, a substitute to the advice given by a counsellor. The content should be regarded as a story about the author's life after divorce. Names were omitted to ensure that this book cannot used to used to identify such individuals and situations have been dramatised for story-telling purposes.

4

Introduction

When my separation happened, it felt like the ground opened up below my feet, and I was ready for it to swallow me whole.

I remember the day so well. But it was an uphill battle towards the divorce that happened (finally!) a few years later. But this book isn't about that. It's about the more positive action you can take afterwards. You *will* go through a period of grieving after the relationship ends. But then you need to lift yourself up and move forward. It was a lesson I had to learn myself.

I'm here to share what I did so maybe your journey is going to be somewhat easier.

The first part of the journey will be like you're mourning. You lost that anchor to a life you may still want to hold onto, but it's better to let it go. If the split was amicable then that's good, but more than often they don't happen in that way, and it will be a period of pain, loneliness and anger.

I can only speak of how it was a woman but evidence shows it's pretty much the same for both parties involved. It hurts. And the pain needs time to go away and for you to heal.

Friendships were what helped me to get over the phase, as well as an understanding mother who'd been through the same. She asked me if I was going to find someone else, and at the time I didn't know. I think it takes time to be ready to move on. You don't want to land into a new relationship 'on the rebound'. It's not fair for that new guy (or gal) and it's not fair to yourself.

Never ever let any person say to you these words: "Get over it."

Getting over a relationship in which you had invested time, effort and love, is hard. Time heals all wounds. An effort is needed to pick yourself up after the mess. And to trust enough to love again needs you to learn to trust in yourself and love yourself first once more. And then you're ready.

<u>Go</u> easy.

Use this book as inspiration. I'm not a relationship expert. But what I *am*, is empathetic to what you're going through. There's no specific order in which to read the chapters. Treat *each* as a bit of 'pick-me-up' as your mood dictates. This book isn't about sorting the finances though I will discuss how I handled, or the divorce process (exclusion of the way it's done makes this a universal book to be read wherever you live) or the pain (I know the pain you feel is real and you need time to recover from the shock a divorce causes).

It's about how to find yourself once more as a person. One of the things my current partner says about *why* he fell in love with me, is that I showed him what sort of person I am. That came from learning to trust in me again and to learn to love myself. Once that happened I was ready for what he offered me.

But not everyone needs to have a second chance at being with a person. This book also assumes that you might want to be on your own. So everything is just as relevant for you in that case too.

There are *twelve* chapters because I gave myself twelve months to go through the process myself. *You* can take as long as you need on each chapter. Feel free to annotate the book with your own thoughts (I've included pages for this purpose at the end of each chapter).

The two blank pages at the end of each chapter are for those thoughts *too*. They're there intentional so you can write down things that come to your mind because you read a chapter.

As stated before, this isn't a self-help book in the traditional sense. It's a mixture of memoir, self-help, self-reflection, storytelling, advice and positive reinforcement. Feel free to annotate OFTEN…

Although the author and publisher have made every effort to ensure that the information in this book was correct at the time it went to press, the author and publisher do not assume and hereby disclaim any liability to any party for any loss, damage, or disruption caused by errors or omissions, whether such errors or omissions result from negligence, accident, or any other cause.

Contents

Chapter One:

Nurture The Mind

Introduction

When you start over with life after a break-up, how do you begin and where?

That was the **first** question mind asked me when my marriage ended. Your mind *will* be messed up; you'll feel lost in this new reality; you'll feel like something has broken deep inside you. Which is actually true as your heart *does* break, even if figuratively.

Even for the person walking away from the relationship, this will be true though they fix it differently, and I'm not going to concentrate on the person who wronged you in this book. My focus is on *you*.

Like me a decade ago, you're asking questions about what to **do** next.

The usual thing I'd hear after my marriage was over, is 'that things would get okay again,' and that I 'would get over the hurt'.

A decade on, most of the hurt is gone, and things got better because I worked on making it *better*. I did most of the work to make it happen **myself**, not by letting others walk in and fix it for me.

In this chapter, I encourage you to look inward at your mindset. You have to let the healing process take its course so you can change your mind's behaviour and attitude to life. Don't listen to people saying to you that you're making it worse by stepping back from life and isolating yourself from life in general. It's easier to find again who you were *before* the marriage if you just let yourself be alone.

The following four chapters I deal with things I generally did to get my mind move from feeling defeat to feeling that I had a chance to overcome and win so I could start over. It's an ongoing process I never stopped.

Even now, as I write this book, I reflect on how my mind changed because what I did or didn't do.

The mind is a tricky part of who we are. I think there's much in the world that influences us into a particular way of thinking. For example, seeing a news report about a terrible event - for me, it was the 9/11 event - does influence how you view the world around you. Witnessing bad events influences your mind and I found myself reflecting often on how I was living my life.

The following questions were often in my mind following that day:

- Is my life worth living in the way I do now?
- What if something similar happens?
- How can I change how I behave around others?
- What if I meet someone new (instead of staying in this relationship)?

We cannot let such questions dominate our minds. It's not good for us when things are normal. When the inevitable day comes when you **do** find yourself alone, you might adopt such mindset but even then it's not good for you. Especially not when you try to deal with a breakup in a way come from it with the as minimal amount of animosity or bad feeling as you can.

Rather than taking a fatalistic approach to deal with a break-up, you can instead nurture your mind; let it **heal** from the pain; **learn** to give yourself a new 'normal'.

It's the above questions I'm going to examine in the four sub-chapters of this chapter. These were questions I asked of myself often during the first days when I was alone. They were tough questions to ask of myself. Tougher than you may realise but in one way or another we all ask these questions when a breakup happens.

Any form of break up as I've realised since, whether it's a lost friendship, a breakdown of marriage, a falling out with a family member, and other similar situations.

Before you start to read the rest of this chapter, turn to the blank pages provided at the end of this chapter and write down there what the number **one** question you're asking yourself right now is.

Your question will sound very different to the questions I asked myself, but when you boil it down to the basics we all ask the same thing: where do I go from here, and how can I create a better life for myself - whether this is alone or with someone new?

Remember also, that you <u>don't</u> have to be with someone new immediately. I'll discuss why and why not in the Friendshipping chapter.

Is my life worth living?

The short answer from the get-go is: **YES!**

Never ever forget that you have to love yourself before *you* can love another person. 'Loving yourself' does mean and does require that you nurture your mind with certain thoughts and a certain type of mindset that fosters positivity.

Even for me, a decade after the divorce, it is tough to feel positive, but I remember something rather interesting from a children's book which has always stuck with me ever since: it is the idea that your mood is like a wheel.

There's a hook on the side of the wheel. The hook picks up things that influence your mind.

It can pick up the bad stuff; this may be the stuff that caused the breakdown of your relationship.

It can also pick up things that make your mind feel better.

When that hook is at the bottom of the wheel, and it's picking up the bad stuff, that's the low point you're working to overcome right now. That's when you need to find the positive things to replace the bad stuff with.

This wheel is ever-turning. It's your mind's opportunity to keep steering it with the hook at the top where it can collect the good things that come your way…

Okay, the book didn't quite explain it in this way, but it's how my mind interpreted it at the time as a child, and the idea of it stuck with me throughout my life. I revisited the concept of the 'wheel' when I had to ask myself whether life is worth living.

The idea here is to reinvent yourself **not** to keep going in the same old way that you did before. A fresh start comes from adopting a new mindset.

For me, a new mindset meant that I had to look at *how* I had been living my life for the decade or so that I'd been married for. Did I do anything then that I could have done differently? This isn't a question that asks if I could have saved the marriage - I couldn't and I knew <u>that</u> back then, and I still know this now.

But, it **does** help to assess how you did things while in the relationship so you can figure out what to do differently now. There's no such thing as a failed relationship being your fault, or even being either person's fault.

Sometimes you end up not being compatible.
Sometimes you just fall out of love.

Any explanations as to why it had to happen should be set aside because that's the other person's very subjective, and possibly also hurt, reasoning talking.

When you fall out of love your wheel is with the hook at the bottom, and you could say things that just make the situation go from what one could consider a 'civil' parting into one where you drag both your families into it (they have **nothing** to do with the private matter of your relationship ending by the way), and you may say things you'll regret later.

Those things you say could be the bad things that attach themselves onto this imaginary wheel and cause your mind to consider your life afterwards to view things differently. In fact, you'll be left wondering if life is worth living the way you do now *or* in the future.

The question I faced, was: Can I cope on my own?

Based on what I did one day, I want you to take a blank sheet of paper and draw a circle on it to represent the wheel, then mark one side with the word 'top' and the other side with 'bottom'. Now draw a large dot on it that represents the placing of the hook. Place this dot wherever you feel it is your 'here and now'.

Let's take this a step further. I often look at my own wheel. In fact, I consider it to be like a clock - hence why there's one on the cover of this book. You know the terms 'clockwise' and 'counter-clockwise'. The left side of the wheel is your 'clockwise' and the right side the 'counter-clockwise'.

Did you put your dot left *or* right, and even more importantly, did you place it above *or* below the 'three o'clock', or above *or* below the 'nine o'clock'?

Placing it above the three o'clock or above the nine o'clock means you have a more positive mindset by nature even with your breakup or even if you want to admit to right now.

Below this position just means you need to give yourself time to heal. Heartbreak isn't over in minutes or hours or even days. It took me over six months to feel a resemblance of confidence, and even when I met that new guy I still had doubt for the first few years.

Even today, as I write this book, I have to admit to myself that I ask myself: "Did I actually meet someone for keeps?"

The answer to that question - for me at least - was and is a resounding YES. But the relationship didn't come easy, was never easy, and I had to teach my guy that I had pain from before. But because he and I believe that the way forward is by communicating often, this pain has dulled over time, and at times I even think: "Yes, this is a **new** me, and I did make things better for me."

Life has its ups and downs, and it's up to you to create as many 'ups' as you can manage. Your mind needs to change how it thinks of you, and if you can get to the answer "YES" in response to the question posed as this subchapter's section then you know your life is heading towards the "up".

In the next chapter, I'll discuss some of how I dealt with my depression in my journey to rediscover myself and to set a new normal for myself.

When you have to deal with that too, the journey to 'up' should begin by making sure you have help with it - ask for help. It's not a sign of weakness doing this, and it can make things so much easier.

I leave you with a few power words:

"You are stronger than you believe you are. Strength comes from recognising that emotions are a relief for the pain you feel. Emotions are not a weakness."

What if something similar happens?

When I met my new guy I was immediately fatalistic about the relationship (unfortunately), though this feeling didn't stay around for long because of the way he was behaving towards me and showing me with actions that I could trust him.

I didn't go as far as sabotaging it but in my Facebook news feed on the real "me", I've seen enough comments from other people who <u>did</u> do things that show they were *or* are sabotaging new relationships, because - as they put it - they're scared they'll be treated the same bad way. I think everything feels this way when they meet new people, whether it's a new friend or a new love interest.

It doesn't have to be that way!

Really!

Yes, I had to convince myself of this truth. I had to convince my mind that this was the way it could **be**; pretty much every day for the first few years after the marriage was over, and even after I had met my new guy.

And *he* had to convince me **too** that these power words applied to me.

So, the similar 'thing' that you think will happen doesn't have to happen if you just take a few steps in your mindset to make yourself stronger.

Remember the power words from the previous sub-chapter. They're pretty much my power words ever since I was told them in the few days after my ex-husband had left.

Power words are words that <u>can</u> help you with coping, but they are also those that empower your mind for change or for growth.

Power words will be things like:

"I can do this…"

"I will succeed with…"

"I can be happy because…"

Create your own list of **ten** phrases to be **your** power words on the blank pages at the end of this chapter.

I hope you DO notice that the words above are affirmations of better things that *can* happen to you. If you *do* meet that new guy (or girl, if you're a guy reading this book), **don't** start with the notion that the relationship is going to fail.

However, it's also important to recognise what went wrong in the previous relationship.

The worst thing you can do is to do the same (or worse) than what had happened before.

In fact, you should **never** start anything with the idea you're going to fail.

If you want to learn something such as, for example, learning to do wall climbing. I've never done it, but if I want to learn it I'm going to tackle it with the mindset that I'll succeed, whether it's immediately, or after a lot of practice.

Or I wanted to **do** something like, for example, write a book such as this one…

In fact, I staked a whole new career on believing that I could succeed.

I did encounter a few mishaps but in the long run, I was in it for the long haul, and also getting affirmations such as "the more you do it, the better you get at it" also helped.

Power words I was told about writing: "The more you do it, the better you'll be."

These words apply to anything you ever do in life.

Also interestingly, if you have one failed relationship you will automatically want to make the next one better.

A better marriage, a better friendship, a renewed relationship with a family member…

If one relationship doesn't work out then **YOU** have the power to change, to make certain you don't make the same mistakes that caused the relationship to end.

Even when it may *not* have been your fault in the first place, you can still learn something from what happened to you AND to be a better person on the flip side.

And remember too, if people don't believe you changed, it's your behaviour and attitude that will prove the opposite.

One of the things I got told several times is 'that I was the same person as I was before' when the individual in question hadn't been around me for several years.

In the chapter 'Family vs Family,' I'll tell you how I dealt with the 'doubters' in my own family who were convinced, from the moment they knew the marriage was over, I'd make the mistake of getting involved with someone similar.

It <u>didn't</u> happen but that never stopped <u>them</u> creating an image of me in their minds of me not changing, being the same person, doing the same mistakes.

It is YOU who makes certain that you change, and no matter what anyone says to you if you know you're changing your behaviour, attitude, personality, etc it's **that** what a 'new guy' (or girl) will see before anything else.

My guy saw it.

I still remember the words he said a decade ago:

"I saw and spoke with someone I can like, even love. I like what I hear because you speak with words of compassion and kindness."

Okay, I'm jumping ahead here when maybe this is part of Find Your Heart chapter, but **this** is proof for me that the change I wanted had come into my life. I worked damned hard to find this 'new me'.

Also, I remember the words my mother stated months earlier:

"Before you can love someone new, you have to know you can love yourself first of all. If you do that, it will attract the attention of someone who will want you for who you are, and not who you were."

In a way, the start of the process of the change I wanted was caused by my mother's words. Yes, I'm convinced that she's the one I must thank each and every day of the rest of my life for what I have *now*.

When I asked myself afterwards, after she'd gone home, the question: "What if something similar happens as before, and I meet a guy who isn't nice or caring, what then?"

The answer came to me only moments later.

I can say NO to having such a person in my life.

I can say NO to having bad stuff happen to me.

At that moment my life started changing.

At that moment my mind started to change how I think about myself.

You can do the same. Right now, are you thinking about how stuff was or how you can make things in the future?

STOP thinking about the past and instead start building your future.

When you were a child you had a dream and aspirations about the sort of life you wanted. Tap into those dreams and use the positive energy from it to decide how your life **WILL BE**.

It will be a better life if you allow yourself to change what you think.

You'll have bad days still as life is never smooth and perfect, but you can influence it in how you look at it.

That 'similar thing' you don't want to happen won't happen if you start doing things differently **right now**!

How can I change how I behave?

Compassion is one of the most powerful components of how we function as a human. It allows us to feel sad when we see someone in pain. It allows us to reach out, and give a person a hug when that person is upset. It will also be what defines you as a generous person in the eyes of others.

When I was at my deepest, darkest moment I was pulled up from that place by something my current guy did. I'm not going into the details of what that something was to protect his, and my, identities, but he did something he didn't have to do.

Especially, because he was fixing the mess left behind when my ex-husband left me.

You know you **have** a compassionate person when he, or she, goes a dozen extra miles to do something *that* big.

Another word for compassion is karma.

Karma is a great deal to me. Oftentimes, I'll say I earn my karma by giving out karma. I guess I found a way to give myself a bit of reversed psychology in this way.

At least, I've decided to convince myself of this over the last decade that this is true.

Believing in something *this* powerful is something that **will** influence you, and in the long run, it **will** change how you see yourself. But more importantly, others will perceive you different too. Some won't but they don't really matter in the greater picture.

Ignore the 'naysayers' who claim you're just delusional because, in the long run, you know you want to change, and if you believe in this wholeheartedly, it will change how you do stuff.

The guy I've been with for the last decade (and I met him after going through the process I described in this book) started to notice that I was changing gradually. Although, I think, in part, this is because I let **him** influence me.

This is something that will happen when (not if) you surround yourself with people who are positive about **you**.

If you're in a positive environment it creates a positive thought pattern that you need to move forward with the rest of your life. The process of 'moving on' is gradual because, as stated before, you do need the time to heal from the pain you feel.

One part of changing things for yourself is to work on acting differently around others. It's tough to do this when you don't know *what* to change. But the internet does make it easier for you.

There are websites where you can find those personality tests, and doing one will show you something about your personality traits, and anything about it that you don't like when you read the results is that 'something' to change about yourself.

So, how do you change your personality, attitudes towards the world, how you do things on day to day basis?

It's easier than you may realise. But it does take some effort.

- Do you have habits you keep repeating?
- How do you react to negative comments?
- Do you keep putting off doing certain activities?

Answering these questions will show you negative traits for your personality. You don't need to do one of those personality tests to determine the answers for these questions.

And getting an answer is the first step towards you figuring out how not to behave around others.

For example, I'll admit that until I started to look at my own behaviour, for the first question the answer for me was that I'd blame *others* for my mistakes.

These days I freely admit that when I make a mistake it's **my** mistake, and <u>no one else</u> caused it. For me, this was the "habit I kept repeating."

The moment I acknowledged I did have this habit, is when I was able to say: *"No, this mistake I just made, is one I caused and no one else."*

When I started to acknowledge this bad trait it's when the change came.

Gradually.

Slowly.

There will be doubters who'll say you never changed. Don't listen to them. Only ever listen to the voice telling you that you <u>can</u> change who and what you are.

The change will be what you believe it to me. If YOU believe it, it happens. It's as simple as that.

Don't assume that this is an indicator that you're acting or behaving in the wrong way while you were in your relationship. It simply means that you do need to acknowledge that something **you** did made him fall out of love, and something he did, caused the same for **you**.

There was something to unbalance the equilibrium that existed between you in the beginning. To create that same environment you have to acknowledge that change is not only needed but wanted too.

So, in the long run, set the doubt aside and go full on into action to be a different person.

You'll amaze yourself every day when you notice you can do this with increased ease. Things WILL get easier over time, even if you feel for weeks or months like life and time stood still for you. If it feels like that it just means your body is telling you to heal more…

What if I meet someone new?

When I met my current guy, I hadn't planned for it to happen.

Not immediately.

And certainly not just one year after my marriage had ended.

We met in a way that I'd never thought as a possible way to meet someone, and I think us getting together both shocked *and* amazed a lot of people.

Many of these same people still know both of us and see our relationship growing in strength every day.

Originally, my thought had been that I would never meet anyone. I just didn't know how to connect with anyone. My thought was a constant stream of doubting.

I had been diagnosed with depression and I felt so low at the time.

But I had the determination to fix stuff. I started working on my process of changing myself two weeks after my ex-husband left. It was mostly grasping straws at first, and I had originally planned to just live my life by myself and not even bother with a new person.

When I met my guy I originally had decided to quit the internet, so to speak.

I had been playing an online computer game which I found *too* boring to play by myself, so I said to myself: *"Just six months more playing this, and then I'm gone from the internet."*

As you may guess that didn't happen…

In February, I met a guy (the person I'm still with <u>today</u> and who will be referred to as "my new guy"), and he and I became friends quite fast. Two months later, and I was starting to regret my plan to go offline for good. Another month later, and he'd managed to make **me** fall in love with **him**.

In fact, the situation was <u>and</u> still is so unique that I'm writing a story based on all of what happened to me but that story is going to be published under my real name, someday at least.

Some of this story is being shared here, and I'm sharing about my life and how I changed my life around under a pen name so not to end up in a court with my ex-husband making unsubstantiated claims about what I may or may not have said in this book. This book is about me after he left not about life with him.

I share the perceptions that my new guy had of me with his blessing because they're as true today as when we met each other for the first time.

So, the next question I started to ask myself was: "What if I meet someone new?"

Then the question quickly became: "What if I meet him and he doesn't like me? What I went through the change for nothing?"

My new guy told me fast enough that he enjoyed talking to me, and that I was an interesting person in his mind. He also started to tell me that he liked me more and more.

Then, I started to like him, even to love him.

But it took me weeks before I could admit this to him, and when I finally could admit it, I blurted out to him I loved him too.

Rather than just saying I liked him, I said: "I love you too…"

This admission from me took both of us by surprise. But I know now that I **had** changed how I saw myself, and what I wanted from life.

It's easy for me to assume that the heartbreak will never go away, but it did, and it will for you—**too**.

It's the direct result of me looking <u>forward</u> rather than looking back, even as hard as that was at times, that caused me to see **hope** where previously I saw *despair*, where I learned that, sometimes, heartbreak **doesn't** last forever.

To overcome the things that put you in a negative mode are tough to overcome, and you will ask yourself often: "What if I meet someone new?"

My answer to you is: "You will if you let yourself do that."

But I <u>know</u> also that this takes time. And <u>time</u> **is** a healing power that makes this possible. It doesn't matter if you meet a person for friendship *or* love.

In fact, friendship in itself is a form of love.

Not the sort of love that puts flutters in your heart, but a love based on trust, a mutual bond of sharing common things.

The **best** sort of love does flow from friendship first. That's why the friendship I forged with my current guy (a decade ago) **was** and **is** the best sort. He tells me today - frequently - I'm *his* best friend.

I have to admit I see him in a similar fashion.

Being in love with your best friend is the **best** sort of love.

So, if you do meet that someone new, work on being friends **first**. Even if it's love at first sight, and you're both head-over-heels in love in just a matter of days, still work on being friends **first**.

Being friends *first* will give the later part of a relationship the renewal any relationship <u>needs</u>.

I'm guessing - and the guessing is only because I'll never get any answers to "Why?" - that the relationship with my ex-husband went stale, because we lost the essence of renewal, after a time.

I *know* I stopped loving him for various reasons, but he never decided to be blunt with me and tell me why without going into all sorts of excuses.

So, I guess we ended up losing the sense of friendship, and I'll leave it at that.

Too often, whenever someone says their relationship has ended, I see them say: "I lost my best friend." But as friendship is a two-way street, the blame…no, that's the wrong word.

The problem of being *less* friendly is something both persons cause whatever the situation may be *or* whatever the cause is.

In the sub-chapter 'New Meaning of 'It Takes Two To Tango' I'll be going over reasons why blaming yourself, or even blaming your 'ex' (whether that be your ex-lover, ex-friend, or the family member you fell out with) isn't the way to cope with everything nor is it the way to move forward.

Blame can easily get in the way of whatever new relationship you're trying to forge.

Because talking about blame will make the new guy (or girl) think that eventually you'll do the same to him or her, and blame them in some way.

Realising this ended up making me *more* thoughtful about what I was saying, and it made me *less* inclined to want to have arguments. Nowadays, I don't like arguments at all. **Not** having any makes me feel more at peace, and it helped forge a better relationship with the new guy I had met, and it means that our relationship has endured in so many ways.

In fact, I believe that the blame game only happens because you deny yourself to want to change.

It doesn't need to be this way and by the end of this book, you realise this is true.

This Page Left Intentionally Blank…
for you to write in.

Chapter Two:

Soothe The Mind

Introduction

As you get in the habit of nurturing your mind, the other component to consider is how to calm the mind, how to be relaxed, and how to be content with a measure of stillness around you.

I'm a believer in meditation and this can take on a different method or manifestation depending on what you believe or what sort of lifestyle you're accustomed to.

To a religious person, this may be through prayer.

A person of another faith will sit with their eyes closed and their mind has drawn inward.

A person with no faith will find their own validation with their own thinking processes.

There is no singular way to go through this process.

To someone else entirely meditation comes from sitting in the warm sun and soaking in the warmth on their face.

Whichever is true, remember that meditation in any form or method is in itself a form of affirmation of 'self.'

It's designed to calm you, to put you in a better place - whether this is spiritual, mentally or emotionally - and come out on the other side with a renewed inner strength.

I do meditation regularly.

For me, it means resetting my mindset to the top of the aforementioned wheel.

For me, it's a time when I **let go** of negative thought or feeling and tell my mind that I'm in a good place, happy, and content with how life is going.

Making sure that you can bring calmness to your mind is as important as nurturing it with a new mindset. These two aspects of the mind feed one another.

As you work on changing your mind, you will also find it easier to calm it whenever something upsets you or whenever life takes a tumble.

I found my own foundations rocked to the core when one day I received an email.

The email came from the mother of a friend I'd been searching for.

The news - most of the details of it I'm going to keep private - was not the good news I had hoped for.

The day the news arrived I retreated into my lowest point, and my new guy (okay, I've had him around for over a decade but to make sure no one ever is mistaken about who I'm talking about I'll keep calling him that in the rest of this book) came home, and found me really upset.

On my wheel, I was at the bottom. Hearing that someone you looked for, is dead, is *not* the sort of thing any of us might cope with.

But the mindset that I have nowadays did something to process it. I decided to meditate, and in the process, I let the memories of the 'good times' heal me as time went by.

Questions I had to ask from myself during this time, were:

- Could I have changed what happened?
- Was my friend happy or sad?
- Did my friend remember me?
- Would my friend have approved of my life?

Yes, the questions you ask while meditating are the very personal questions that the practical part of nurturing your mind will want to omit.

Now, in the blank pages at the end of this chapter write down 3-5 questions about some sort of event you've experienced, other than your break-up, that **you** feel had an impact on your life in general (it can be a childhood event or something more recent).

The questions should all be related to the same event.

After finishing this book, go *back* to those questions and see if your mindset has changed about whatever you wrote down.

I'll tell you that months of meditation and thinking things over has changed *how* I see the above questions now.

There was *no* way I could have done anything to change what happened.

It was my friend's life and therefore she would have decided to live it her way.

As stated in the last chapter, the choice to change comes from yourself alone so you can tell a person a million times to be different, if they don't want it they won't change.

Similarly, you can assume a million times like a broken record someone will never change, if they change you have to accept it as a fact that it happened.

I have a photo of my friend as she was as an adult.

In the photo, I see a happy person so I'm convinced she **was** happy for part of her life at a minimum. I have no right to assume she was sad at the end of her life.

I should presume that she had a happy life.

I remembered my friend.

From what I got told about her I *have* to assume she remembered me *too*.

The last question was the hardest one to ask me.

I will guess that there would have been an equal sense of urgency of helping if she'd found me first and had realised about my previous marriage, but I can never know if she would have approved.

That choice was gone when I got the news.

I often will just guess that she'd helped me the pain of divorce, and then she would have told me that changing how I am as a person is the best thing to do.

But now I'm just guessing and that's never good.

So, I'll just leave it with an "I hope so…".

Meditation and Self-Reflection

Meditation and self-reflection aren't the same things but they **do** have a close relationship.

In meditation, you'd work on learning to find a calmness in your mind and your overall state of well-being, whereas self-reflection, you're letting the rational side of you examine who and what you have become, decide whether this is who you want to be, and how you want to move forward from this point onward.

That's my view of both of these ways of finding peace in your mind.

That's pretty much my takeaway of how all the websites individually seem to explain this topic.

For me, meditation means that I just have a period of stillness.

Not just is the house quiet but I just let my mind drift as I stare out of the window and look at the tops of the trees moving in the wind, at the clouds drifting by, at the sound of birds chirping or a dog barking in the distance.

I don't concentrate on analysing my mind, or on what's going on in my life or anything.

If it's happening it happens on a subconscious level where I'm not aware of it.

Feeling that zone of stillness around me is a perfect way to allow my mind to **heal** any pain it feels from the little bit of heartache which still wants to rear up from time to time.

Oftentimes, I feel definitely better afterwards.

Sometimes, I will just go into this mode of meditation while I sit curled up in the arms of my current partner.

Being in a nurturing environment of being embraced by someone who loves you, is in itself a form of meditation or even perhaps self-reflection.

When you're in this place of solace it also allows you to think. My new guy will usually let me just talk if I then feel the need to talk about something.

Talking is a release of whatever bubbles up when you are in this mode of meditation and/or self-reflection. It's not the only way for you to release whatever comes to the surface.

Art and music, whether doing it or enjoying it can also help with the release.

I bet you've had those moments where you felt in the mood for a certain type of song, or to look at certain types of photos or artworks, or that you find you're in the mood for a certain type of movie to watch.

All these are contributory to the release of your inner feelings.

When you listen to your favourite song or music it allows you to drift off, when you look at certain types of photos or artworks you can place yourself in them almost like you're in a story and the same goes with movies.

In fact, colour does also play a factor in self-reflection. They relate directly to our mood as an individual.

As an example, I used red, black, white and some beige/grey on the cover for this book. In terms of the typical psychology of colours, red will represent passion or love.

This is a book about finding out whether you can love again which is why I added the colour red to the cover. Black, at least to me, represents loss, whereas white can represent innocence.

Beige or grey is supposed to be emotionless but I think it's more the colour representing change.

I've always believed that there's a link between our emotions and the sort of colours we are exposed when we're in a particular emotion.

Red is a positive emotion but it can also be used in a rather negative way.

When you're angry, it's better to sit down around soft colours or white and remember I just said it represents innocence.

In the colour wheel, as used by an artist, the *more* white that's added to a primary colour such as red, green, blue, yellow, orange or purple, the fewer of the **stronger** emotions are expressed when using the subsequent colour.

You have the contrast of black and red on the cover of this book, so you have the direct representation of loss, e.g. heartbreak.

The fact that it is followed by the affirmation of it not lasting forever and the red represents finding new love, a new friendship, renewal, and finding a new strong emotion in a more positive way.

Self-reflection is a positive activity that does the same thing as looking at colour for a positive message.

Like the red replacing black, therefore renewal replacing loss, you replace despair with a content inner voice of positive reinforcing messages.

So, when you do meditation be aware of **where** you do it.

Understanding colour (which I will go into briefly in the subchapter **Art As Therapy**) will give you the tools to make meditation, and your time for self-reflection, as good as it can get. But I'll explain a little bit here using one example.

Pink is a variant of the colour red.

As a colour, it has been shown to have both the passion to start over as well as the means to find that original feeling of innocence you might have felt when you were in love for the *first* time with that guy who has now broken your heart.

Self-reflection alone can give you time to find the innocence once more.

My new guy often tells me something I find rather appropriate. He thinks that it is the real "me" just thinking about *what* I want and *then* telling him what's on my mind… as I said at the beginning of this subchapter it's what allowed *him* to understand **me** better.

Before you accuse me of not talking to my 'ex,' which was so different as he didn't want to listen because the "chatterbox" part has always been that way.

And because I was so into reading books as a kid I never noticed I always was this way until someone (my new guy) came along who appreciates me for all the talking that I do…

Self-reflection leads to **this** sort of way of thinking.

Oh, and even if pink or red isn't your favourite colours, and another colour is YOUR favourite colour you can STILL assign a positive feeling to the colour.

For example, if green is your favourite colour it represents to **you** the same thing I said earlier about red and pink.

It also **can** create the same positive feeling associated with self-reflection and renewal in the SAME way…

I guess perhaps that's why some people talk to their plants. Yes, I'm convinced that's another form of self-reflection or meditation.

The takeaway of all this is for you to find something in your mind that connects you back to the days when you felt positive when you felt hope when you felt you could take on the world.

When you find this, that's when you have conquered yet another little part of this feeling of 'giving up' after a breakup.

Here are a few more power words for you:

Your mind is a tool that makes you feel better again. The mind has its own way of solving a dilemma you struggle with...

Mind Over Mind

When you want to change you can influence your mind into a different mindset. This is tied closely to personality traits and general ways of thinking.

It's something that suddenly "struck me" one day on a cold November day. If I did things differently my mind would also be different.

This is why I don't believe to dwell - EVER - on the opinions others might have of you. Yes, you have to prove to them that you're different but actions DO speak louder than words ever can.

If *they* believe you to be a quitter then do something from **beginning** to the **end** of the project - it can be a small project but you can demonstrate you are NOT a quitter.

On completion, you'll have changed your mind with your own mind. Your mind pushed you on, and in doing so, you changed your mind.

I call this "mind over mind" action. It's something I decided to give this name, not to be special in some way but by just wanting a name for it.

I needed to give the **change** I was attempting to affect ME a *name* of some sort, and that's the name I gave it.

Other people have another way of describing this process but this is how I referred to it when I started to realise I was trying to change something about how I viewed me.

I had hoped that those who were the closest to me, that being my direct family and the few friends I had from those days would also notice it.

But to the friends, it matters more they were listening to whatever my 'ex' said about the divorce. *They* decided to believe him.

I guess, and I'm just guessing now, that even if I met one of them right now in the street they would assume I'm still the same person they knew based on an assumption put in their head by whatever my 'ex' said.

This is also why taking sides or even being involved while a break-up goes on isn't good. It's no good for the two people breaking up. It's also not good for you either because if you share a friendship with two people, and then they break up you are ultimately left to choose a side.

Although, if you don't ask for details of how or why the relationship ended, you have none of those decisions to make.

But this all is something for that friend or other third parties to solve.

However, that said. You can make things easier for that other person by telling them to stay out of the situation for now. You work on changing who you are.

And then, that person will notice it and take notice. It can **act** as a defence against whatever an 'ex' *may* say of **you**.

But now I'm digressing from the topic of this subchapter.

The mind needs to change when it's affected by something traumatic such as the end of a relationship.

This is also applicable when you lose a job, when someone passes away, when you lose a beloved pet, or when you have to face the upheaval of moving from one place to a new place.

There are too many traumatic and less traumatic things that can happen to us.

Some of them are more stressful than others.

But switching to the other end of the spectrum, something like a wedding can be as stressful, and so is having a baby. The change associated with these affects a person in a different way.

But they still cause a change in the mind to happen.

This is where I feel the mind over mind action can work for people in any situation. You want to look at how life is becoming when the change happens so you can cope with the change whether it's a better change (like getting married) or not-so-good stuff, like a divorce, a loss of friendship or loss of a loved one.

Now for the bit of magic of changing your mind.

You do this by making a list of habits.

Are any of them, things that feel odd?

Those habits may be the things you need to reevaluate.

I made a list each morning of what I'd perceive to be my habits on a paper, then I would fold it and store it away. As I do stuff in a day I'd write down on another piece of paper what I had done.

This can be…snacked at 10.30 AM, argued with someone calling me at 11 AM, skipped lunch in favour of biscuits, etc.

Yes, these are actually examples of *bad* behaviour I used to have a decade ago when I started on the path to change myself.

Yes, this is very much liking a list of New Year's resolutions every day.

But if you want to change yourself you have to force it on you.

The list made in the morning is a list of things I wanted to do, achieve or accomplish.

For me, it was important not to snack all the time. It was a bad habit I developed because of how my 'ex' behaved towards me.

By stopping this habit I would remove the object of his criticism from my life. It means that if he claimed "she's always like this" the people who'd meet me after I made my changes could say "No!".

Arguing was a daily occurrence in the marriage so it was important to remove this behaviour from my daily life.

You might have heard of the words: *"Think before you speak."*

In changing how you **talk** to other this becomes a key virtue to pursue. You don't need to look at this even in any negative way, as often is done, because usually it's used as a criticism.

Thinking before you speak is a way to *learn* the "mind over mind".

If you know the precise words to say and know to say them so there is no anger in your voice, that you show respect to the listener, and you show constraint, it actually gains you respect.

Last time ever I spoke to my 'ex' I SPOKE and did raise my voice **once**.

Inside my mind, I was seething with obvious anger directed at him. But the funny thing about the situation was that by having learned the constraint and learned to be different in my mindset I was in control and I was the one who could make the demands for him to leave me alone.

Not realising that I could CHANGE actually scared **him**. And his behaviour made it clear to me that he needed to be in control and being stronger, more assertive, etc took the control away from him, and put it back in my hands.

People can be scared when you portray yourself as an empowered person. However, being empowered and projecting this only means you have gotten to where you wanted to get to with the "mind over mind" change you started on. It's not something to happen overnight, or in a week or anything like it. It took me at least four years to get out of the self-imposed "I'm a victim" mindset to shape to the self-assured mindset I have.

The person who benefited from the changes I made is the new guy. And because I communicate often with him he probably knows me better than my 'ex' ever did…

That's the end goal you're working on now that you found out that heartbreak, loss or change in your circumstances doesn't need to keep you there in the darkness.

Reach for the light at the end of the tunnel, and start **living** again… like I have done, and keep doing each and every day as I move forward to a better life…

Finding Yourself Again

It is easy to forget in a relationship that you have your **own** identity, especially when it's one that goes from okay to bad.

This can happen for any number of reasons. As stated in the last chapter it's never one or the other person's fault that things go bad and end in a relationship.

Sometimes, people just fall out of love or fall, or out of friendship, etc. Just like in a job there *can* come a day *when* the job you do, feels like you've outgrown it; in a relationship, you *can* outgrow the feelings you once had.

When that happens that's when it's time to start finding yourself again.

After a few years of self-imposed changing how I did things and what way I spoke or interacted with people around me, I was so ready to find ME again.

I was reminded, a week or so after my 'ex' had left me to "be the person you were as a child, the person who dreams and hopes for the future, and someone who would see the best in people around her."

One day I woke up, looked at myself in the mirror and had the mindset of "I can do this."

The process to get there took me four years.

It took a few more years longer to get to a point in my life where I ended up "becoming an author", and even if this process is slow it is guided by the "mind over mind" principle I developed for myself as stated in the previous subchapter.

When you outgrow a relationship you may forget you have a "self" that had been attractive to the other person…once. And then boom it can be gone.

I was watching a movie weeks ago, before finalising the edits on this book. The scene shows a woman walking along a street and then she sees her ex.

The exposition in the movie made it clear who he was. Her reaction to him, especially when his new love interest walks out of the store, was a classic reaction. She was all swagger and saying she's okay, but then when she turns and walks off you can see she was upset. That next moment, the turning point in the movie is the moment that character was starting to find herself again…

It is a **similar** process in real life.

When you walk from the failed relationship, or the person you were with does, either of you will do so full of swagger.

But I don't look at my past relationship as a failed relationship any more.

Why not?

The answer is so simple.

Life is all about learning **new** things and about coping with new situations.

The idea of "being set in your ways" is old-fashioned to me, even if I'm somewhat conservative and traditional - yes, I **do** believe that a man can hold a door open, but at the same time, I also think it's very possible for him to help with cooking an evening meal.

Being conservative or traditional doesn't really mean you *have* to go along with the traditional model of doing things.

If your mind tells you that doing things different includes holding a door open for a man (as a woman) then just DO it.

And if, as a guy, you want to help with cooking, the simplest things such as putting out the plates and cutlery, retrieving a baking dish from the oven or draining the boiling rice is helping.

You don't need to be a master chef to help the person you live with, and in a way, this sort of behaviour will also benefit the children you have living with you.

A role model is not just someone who behaves by taking that "manly role".

He can also show the children that in a relationship the two people sharing a life are equal.

This is what my new guy showed me and he wanted this because of how he viewed me with my changes in my mindset.

So, the easiest way to find yourself, in my opinion, is to be allowed to BE yourself in any new relationship. *If* the person you meet was in a previous relationship, and he or she was hurt by it and is making an effort to improve who they are, you can help them with it and help them to become the new 'self' they might be striving to become.

The easiest way to find yourself is when your heart isn't being broken any more.

Let the new love you will meet eventually do the remaining of the healing, and therefore give you the means to be YOU again…

Mind Management

A healthy mind is created by different factors in your life, even if some of them are things we cannot control directly. However, that said, you can influence your mind in a **few** ways.

Okay, it may be that you struggle with such stuff as depression, anxiety or other conditions.

I deal with depression and anxiety as a consequence of the way my marriage had gone.

But, it **doesn't** stop me working on calming the mind, on keeping it healthy and strong, and it certainly isn't used to dwell on the negativity and pain that had been caused.

Now, immediately, you ask me: *"How do you keep 'the mind' strong, huh? It ain't a muscle..."*

True. It's not a muscle.

It's a grey mass consisting of a whole load of fluid with all these weird synapses firing off to create memories, digest memories, process memories and whatever else a brain is supposed to do.

I use **my** brain to write books… lots and lots of them I hope…

I think about things.

In the process of thinking, learning, watching the news, reading books, talking with other people, listening to a bird chirp, throwing a stick for your dog, or cooing at your newborn baby… all of these are methods where **YOU** make your mind strong.

It's the process of learning that enriches your skill and knowledge of the world we live in.

It's when you talk to a neighbour when you start forming new opinions (or improving older ones).

It's when you interact with a pet you leave behind some of the worries.

They say owning a dog is **good**.

Right now, I don't have a dog. Hopefully, I will own one again one day…

I once owned a dog, and to prevent anyone linking this book with my real identity, I'll call the dog "**Bob**" in this next story.

This is <u>one of the few times</u> in this book you get an insight into what my married life was like - it also explains **why** I'm writing this book with a different pen name other than my own.

Anyway, Bob was adopted when my marriage was already on the rocks.

Okay, screeching to a halt in this story (in that typical cliche sort of way sometimes used in movies) because you ask me **now** WHY I didn't leave the marriage at **that** moment instead of later on when, as the saying goes, the shit hits the fan… (the same question does occasionally pop up in my mind too even today).

I guess the answer is that I didn't know yet **THEN** how bad things would become.

Bob was a beautiful dog. He'd sleep beside me when I was working on my hobbies (Check the **Go Creative** chapter for why art is so good in dealing with depression).

Then, the trouble in the relationship became a "loud verbal explicit."

I guess I don't want to list what was said to prevent the 'ex' from being able to sue me over this book if ever he discovers it.

Yes, it even takes a lot of courage even to write it under an assumed name, but that's why I started to focus on the word "strong" in my explanation above.

So, to continue my story, my dog Bob wouldn't have any of my 'ex' behaving in this way towards me…

He'd sit up and come really close to my side. In that ultra-protective sort of way that dogs may do when they feel a human is at risk in their version of what risk means.

As time went on he became increasingly protective of me, and yes, he'd growl at times **when** the "loud verbal explicits" came.

I guess he recognised some threat in the voice saying those words.

The 'ex' **didn't** like this at all…

But I think *this* process of my dog being protective of my well-being, **is** what allowed my mind to start changing.

From a mind wanting to *feel* vulnerable and weak, from a mind that was blaming *me* for the situation I was in. To a mind that knew I could start **to stand up for myself.**

Bob **taught** me something about how **all** dogs (and related species) act. They look out for the **weakest** in their pack. They don't leave a member of their pack behind…

This realisation altered how I viewed the world. It started to make me a **fighter** for justice, equality and fairness.

Bullying is **high** on my list of the **no-no's** that I wanted to be different in life as my real "me."

So, from a small friendship with a dog, I managed to go from weak to **strong** in my mind.

Personally, I'm also convinced that dogs are the perfect companion to teach a child about good friendships. Dogs live in the moment, and they **are** super-loyal. If you can get a dog, get one to allow your child to find that same strong mind as I did back then.

When your mind is in a good place it's going to feel healthier.

Even if you battle **every day** with depression and anxiety if you **do** things to benefit your worldview towards a more **positive** outlook you help yourself.

In the chapters, **Finding Help By Helping Yourself** and **Intro Going Outro** I go into what I did to find a *more* positive outlook myself. On the blank page following this chapter write down things you think **will** make your mind stronger.

These, typically, are things you know you're good at already. Concentrating on things you're good at is often better than trying to figure out new things to learn.

Yes, this **strongly** contradicts what I said earlier, in the previous chapter, about changing **how** you behave *but* the behaviour is a different construct than skill and that's why skill **can** be altered.

Make your mind stronger by doing what you already do best.

For example, I've often been told - the real "me" that is - that I'm empathic. So, I thought a book about what causes me to be that way would be a good thing to write.

In part, the ability to express much more empathy came about, first of all, from learning it from **Bob**.

Later on, as I started to analyse what I had to **do** to change my life, this new philosophy on life got affirmed by my new guy in terms of what he said to me: "I saw something in you that makes you a kind, caring person."

Putting strength into your mind may not solve such things as depression or anxiety BUT it will make you be a person you'd want to be. Embracing the limitations of your emotions makes you **more** compassionate to the needs of others.

And thus, you became strong...

This Page Left Intentionally Blank…
for you to write in.

Chapter Three:

Finance Is A Big Step

Introduction

I'm not going to beat around the bush. Sorting out your finances when you were **two of you**, and now it's just you **on your own**, is tough. It requires a lot of discipline to cut back.

The first thing that needs to be tackled is debt. Stacks and stacks of it. Some of it may result from splitting up 'joint finance' into two parts.

Taking over the responsibility of some or all those bills can be costly.

The other person, in some cases, may dispute they have any responsibility to pay off part of the debts.

When in doubt you make sure you record you paid for something and that you have the proof for it. This way the other person cannot claim to have paid and they cannot claim either that you never paid.

This chapter isn't about what to sort out because everyone has different bills and financial arrangements. This chapter is more about the mindset - yes, this is my favourite word in many ways (bursts into song singing 'Money Makes The World Go Round'… errr, perhaps not). But you get the idea.

If you have a healthy mindset and attitude you can FIX the situation you may find yourself in after a break-up.

There are three parts of this mindset I tackled when I found myself with not even enough money for a loaf of bread in my purse. And no money in the bank.

Yet, through sheer determination and also some help I was able to turn around the situation I was in and go from broke to **not** broke, though I won't say I'm wealthy. That's the part of this stuff I'm still working on. It's why I decided to get into book writing as a job. And yes, writing is a job that requires discipline, resilience and a drive to never give up.

You can look at successful authors with a thriving career as the reason why I write and why I don't want to give up.

More about creativity will be covered in the **Go Creative** chapter.

Remember what I said in the last chapter. How it is the change by doing the "mind over mind" technique I suggested that changes your attitude towards things. Finance, along with other things such as food, your interactions with family and how you feel about yourself are all things affected by the change in your mind.

But by changing your attitude towards finance, which means you need to cut out the things you cannot afford, or if needed skimp on it. I still skimp on things.

I have the "bare necessities" in terms of financial stuff.

The income from my writing is making *tiny* dents into financial needs.

I'm going to measure the success of my writing in terms of being self-reliant 100% without needing help from my new guy in any way.

When I start contributing equally to the household income needs that's **when** I know I'm reaching my goal.

And yes, I've decided I might need a job for it unless my writing career suddenly took off in a major way, and that's why I admire authors who have managed to do this so much.

Also never feel jealous of a genuinely successful person. He or she has worked hard to get to where they are now. And be honest and genuine with earnings because there comes a feeling of satisfaction of "I did this" when you earn your own money…

A Penny For Your Thought!

This is one of my favourite expressions, however, for the purpose of this book I decided to make it singular instead of how it is usually written: "thoughts."

It means that someone wants to know what you are thinking. Your thoughts are a commodity really that you could use to make your life better, easier or nicer.

A thought could land you your **next** job if you decided to go for one.

So, what are you thinking right **now** about your life, and maybe about the reason *why* you wanted to buy and read this book?

Was the reason because you had a break-up and you needed to find a way to sort out your thought processes, perhaps process the pain you're feeling, and find some sort of book to help you get over it all?

Write those thoughts down at the end of this chapter. They will be a big factor in how you work on the rest of the stuff to change it.

From a personal viewpoint I've noticed I will, at times, get really thoughtful, pensive, drawn inward. It's in these moments that my own mind will say "a penny for your thought" to get me out of these moments.

As stated at the beginning of the book there are times when I just sit beside my new guy and talk about whatever is on my mind no matter what the topic might be.

When you start a new relationship I urge you to discuss finance. Because talking about it openly normalises it and makes it less contentious and less of something you could argue about.

Finance can be discussed between two equals without needing to raise one's voice, without getting angry, and by being honest with it you avoid almost all associated problems people typically have in their relationship with one another.

My new guy and I often talk about what we'd do if we won the lottery, what we do with income from book sales, with income from his job and I generally tell him at least once a week that I want to find a job I can do.

That **is** the positive side of talking about finance. It **can** bring two people closer. But I also know it can cause people to grow apart and have issues, and how you tackle this topic does all depend also on your upbringing, but again I say to you that you **can** change this mindset along with every other.

Finance is a fickle thing to get right especially if you don't have a brain for numbers.

Finances, in general, are complex to get right, especially if you want to save up for the future (see the subchapter **Future-Proofing** for ideas).

The easiest way to get started before you do any number crunching you want to make a list of the things you want from life.

When you've figured this out, you can start number crunching. You want to work out what's the need for weekly, monthly and annual costs. Make sure to include the cost of any hobbies and if you plan to run any form of business you need to account for that **too**.

Don't be afraid to ask for help in organising your finances if you need such help. Banks and other reputable financial institutes can help you with advice and planning. In addition, the tax office (the IRS in the USA, HMRC in Britain, Skatteverket in Sweden as a few examples) can be good sources for information and advice too. If you live in another country just contact your own tax office.

I would be careful of online sources of unofficial advice but also online suggestions for making a quick buck. These "get rich quick jobs" are no jobs. There's no such thing as earning an income without putting something into it as effort.

And yes, that even applies to book writing.

Only a **few** authors of the millions publishing every year make a living wage. A lot of people I know personally need second and/or third jobs besides their writing career, and in some cases, I've seen people having to give up writing to an additional job.

But it is also something where you can reach that life of comfort if you work at it. This is what I put on my *own* list of things I wanted to get done.

So, a penny for your thought now you know how I changed how I dealt with and viewed money. For me, now, every penny counts. If I can get something done cheaper it will give me more money for something else.

So, be precise with your finances, budget for a much longer period. I do it typically for the next decade altering the numbers if there are changes.

Be transparent with finances, both to yourself and those around you...

Organising Is a BIG Thing

Besides organising my finances there are several other things I decided to organise in the first few years after my 'ex' had gone. You're familiar with the expression "doing a spring clean."

That's precisely I decided to do.

It wasn't easy and it took time.

But the situation was somewhat comical looking back. And to set it up I'm going to use a little bit of healthy exposition…

I used to live in a flat in Britain, and there are these "wheelie bins" that are used for refuse.

If not familiar with Britain it's a slender dark-grey rubbish bin that the local refuse collection service collects. These bins typically can take 5-6 rubbish bags. In Britain, people may typically use 'bin liners' that are 30-litre black plastic bags though some can be bigger or smaller. There were about ten of these wheelie bins outside the building with the flats…

Now I've set up the situation I'll continue with my story about doing a spring clean.

My 'ex' had left a whole load of junk and useless stuff behind. I had a walk-in cupboard in the house and, first of all, I dumped **all** the content I considered **not** to be mine or useful to me in the cupboard.

I was literally more than knee deep IF I wanted to into the cupboard.

I immediately knew, also, that having the junk *there* would be considered a fire hazard if the landlord decided to do a spot inspection.

I asked the neighbour who did know of my situation if I could 'borrow' a few bin liners, and then showed the junk. He ended giving me a whole unused roll of bin liners and told me to consider it as a 'gift.'

I now had forty 30-litre bin liners. In addition, I had also found a couple of shopping bags filled to bursting capacity with more shopping bags a day later inside one of the kitchen cabinets. Their use would follow…later on.

I started to fill up the bin liners, but because I was uncertain if my 'ex' might turn up whenever I would go to deposit a filled bag I would lock my front door. Strangely enough, I switched from doing this work during the day to doing it at 4 am. I was late summer and still relatively light at this time of the day. I started on the day after the rubbish was collected…

So, the first eight bags - I managed to cram eight bags into a wheelie bin designed to only take an average of six, somehow - went into the furthest wheelie bin, and then I worked my way closer to my building of flats.

It took three days but at the end, the bins were **all** filled completely.

And then I'd be really funny by leaving the house with filled up shopping bags to fill ALL the bins at the two *other* building of flats a few dozen yards walking distances from my house.

There was a LOT of junk, and after this escapade of filling up everyone's bins over a total of four days - I don't even know if **anyone** noticed even though the neighbour knew I had the bin liners - but this is where things get funny.

Really, really funny.

(Injects humour into a book that otherwise would be boring)

Someone *obviously* called the landlord and they organised an extra refuse collection on Monday (day 5) and that just prompted me to continue with removing junk and depositing bin liners packed to bursting point into the wheelie bins.

By the "regular" refuse collection day ALL the bins, except for half of wheelie bin number **10**, were filled up once more. I did see other people's rubbish in bags beside the bins that morning…

I decided to call it 'spring cleaning' and also down-sizing so not to feel guilty about what happened to the bins. But the end result was magical. I already had fewer furniture as a result of my 'ex' leaving, but for the first time ever I had space in the flat.

This had an added bonus as having a more spacious environment with a down-sized feeling to it CAN also make you feel less claustrophobic which is a possible symptom you feel when you have anxiety.

This had an immediate effect on how I viewed my work ethics.

It caused me to become more organised with data on my PC though being really organised in this respect is still an ongoing thing but I did make certain to as organised with the business side of my life that being everything to do with book writing. Or, at least, as much as I can be.

Being organised makes life a whole lot simpler and better. You know where you keep your bills and statements. You know where your personal paperwork is kept. You have less cleaning to do which frees up time for other things (such as hobbies, and this is what lead me to write as a career in the first place).

Being organised at home can also influence your work too. Being organised with clothing and personal hygiene gives you a body image. If you have children you influence them in a positive way.

If you meet a new person you influence them with it too, and most of the time in a good way.

So, even though, it's a big thing to get organised (and it can take a considerable amount of time to actually DO it), the resulting effect caused by it is much bigger.

So, actually, it's a SMALL thing compared to the end result that **you** get from it in so many parts of your life…

Future-Proofing

In relationships, we often don't count on having to put in place security for the future because most of us think that when we find the "love of our life" it will keep going for life.

But you need to assume you need to have to take care of yourself at any time in any relationship.

Not for negative reasons.

But simply because it's something that can happen…

I call it future-proofing but I didn't invent the term. I'm simply borrowing it from the source where I heard it first.

Actually, the context in which I heard it originally was in a business-related context, and to make sure you get finance back on track after a break-up you **do** have to treat it as a business pretty much because you need to plan, budget and organise in a similar way as you'd have to be for a business.

We all have heard the way the Royal Family in Britain is referred to as 'The Firm'.

They actually do a small aspect of family management **well** in using such a regimented system of looking after themselves.

They plan and regulate everything to do with their finances (according to a programme I saw on television).

In a way, you need to become as strict if you want to get back on track with finance, too.

Maybe, I'm a total amateur next to *The Firm*, but I took notes about what they DO, and I've tried to adapt my life to become more disciplined so that, eventually, I can get similar results (on a smaller scale) as *they* do.

An easy example of where such changes can be made is in terms of what food you purchase.

Fresh produce *can* last longer, *is* healthier, but also if you spread it over a few weeks of planning meals **will** come out cheaper.

And **don't** forget that being healthier also makes health cost cheaper.

The <u>end goal</u> you have to set for yourself is two-fold:

1) You need to get a source of income with a job or business. As you can tell by *this* book I made my job to be that of being an author. It's **not** an instant income source, nor easy to get yourself known as an author. You have to be naturally resilient, determined and **not** afraid to stop yourself from giving up. So get a job that suits you and work hard.

2) Establish an evergreen income source for yourself. This *is* a bit trickier as you need to research what is the best sort of work for you to do. Examples of this are doing good podcasts on YouTube, doing game streaming a few time a week on a streaming service such as Twitch, set up a savings account, create a stock photo contribution account somewhere (such as Shutterstock). Again you have to work hard at it, but anything you set your mind to CAN be done…

Creativity and working on making life better for yourself go hand in hand here. Sit down and list each and every skill you have.

You're **not** making a Curriculum Vitae (CV), but instead, you're making a simple list of things you know, things you can do, etc so perhaps a resume *may* do in this situation.

Remember that making a budget for the weekly shopping **is** a skill you can add to the CV or resume.

Places such as Skillshare and similar sites can teach you new skills, and YouTube has tons of videos to give you new knowledge too.

Every new bit of knowledge you possess makes your future more future-proofed. Someone will want this knowledge, and then you can create the means to make your life much better, more secure, and be more independent financially.

In fact, the memoir I decided to write in this book is the accumulation of the knowledge I set out to learn to future-proof my life. I still do this every day.

And if, like me, you **did** get writing your own books you are making yourself known to create believable stories or informative non-fiction.

Saving up money is definitely another way to future-proof your life.

If you keep two or more sources for savings you can make certain that you can save up for different things you may want, or that you might need.

When you start to save up, first make certain you have **all** the regular bills covered.

From the money left over, you split it into the following portions: 50/35/15 per cent, into long-term, medium term and short-term savings portions.

Long-term saving could mean, for example, you save up for bigger expenses (such as a new fridge freezer if you end up needing one, or if you can to move to a new place of residence).

The medium-term is the more expensive things such as new clothing for a job or possibly to do a few hobbies. Short term is for extra bills that might pop up.

Another future-proofing method is to look at ways that you could earn extra income.

One of these methods that are becoming more and more popular is to start a YouTube channel.

If you have a cell phone you can even start doing your videos on the cell phone (according to what some of the YouTubers I watch say).

As the income from having the YouTube channel grows, you can buy a few gadgets to improve (also add these to the medium and/or long-term goals).

Photography for doing high-quality photos so you can add them onto stock photo websites, such as Shutterstock, is another good long-term future-proofing idea.

So is writing books, by the way, because almost all authors don't find instant success and you have to do it for the long haul.

However, when you write a book, make sure you get it **edited**, and then once it's for sale it can stay for sale **indefinitely**.

Don't EVER pay for having a book published as that's vanity publishing, and can be regarded as a SCAM. And a very, very costly one based on certain sites out there who suggest success can be "bought" in exchange for tens of thousands of Dollars or Pound Sterling. So the easiest way to determine if it's a scam…if they want your money up front, it's a scam. This applies to all those "multi-level marketing companies" out there TOO!!!

The publishing process, these days, can be done through "print on demand" websites such as the Ingram Spark and/or Kindle Desktop Publishing (I used these to produce my books independently). The only immediate investment you **do** need to make besides the best editing you can afford is to get your ISBNs.

In the USA, you purchase them from Bowker. For other countries, you need to locate your local ISBN agency.

As copyright *can* be inherited by your extended family I personally call book-writing a 'generational future-proofing effort'. An example of the latter is what Agatha Christie *did* when she created a limited company in Britain. Her family *still* controls the rights to her works this way, and that ensures a much longer return to the initial investment.

Other examples of future-proofing are the pursuit of art, offering online classes and, though with some risk attached, investing. If you look around you will likely find more examples.

If working on future-proofing yourself just be sensible about **what** you do and **how** you do it.

An advert in a shop offering "envelope stuffing" is a **scam** and DOES NOT give you *any* form of future-proofing.

Before I move on, remember that online versions such as "multi-level marketing" (MLM) or completion of surveys are also scams and should be avoided as well.

Most of these schemes prey on vulnerable people, and when you come from a broken relationship you **are** vulnerable. So keep your money for better things, educate yourself to become business-minded in your own right, and build a proper legitimate business from the ground up if you want to go down that route.

New Job, New Everything

Getting a new job can both be exciting and terrifying. It can be the best day of your life or it can be the day when you regret your decision and you can't wait for the next job to come along.

At first, you may not have a choice in the type of job you go for because you have to start somewhere with an income.

When you get the new job it will give you the chance to learn new skills. Stick with it long enough (like a year or whatever) to give you skills you can take with you into the next job.

The goal, obviously, is to become more employable.

But what happens *if* you don't get a job immediately?

It doesn't stop **you** from learning and gaining skills *if* you learn at websites, such as Skillshare and other similar websites. I personally regard my own learning process to be a lifelong endeavour.

There is **always** something new to learn or find out, etc.

As an author, I do something else that's interesting, and that's to do a huge amount of research.

This is one reason **why** being an author is so much fun. Most of my 'wisdom' that resulted in me changing who I am caused the reasoning that then resulted in *this* book, comes from this other learning process.

There's a funny comment I'll often see in my social circles, and that is: "Oh no, what will people think of my browsing history" (or variants thereof).

*Yeah, actually, when you're writing books you DO get a lot of browsing of some sort with rather **odd** stuff in it.*

The funniest these references are to see someone do an "asking for a friend" request for methods of "how one might mutilate a part of a guy that's most sacred to him"

(This was an author's precise words on Facebook - I won't name the author in question but, if ever, she read this book she'd know these precise words came from her...I laughed so hard at the question and answers suggested to her alike...)

I don't think I laughed as hard as reading the hundred or more comments to the post and then adding my own.

*Okay, admittedly **that** post was made on one April Fool's Day but it was very hilarious really. I do have a good, and somewhat wicked, sense of humour. That part of me decided it was the BEST April Fool's Day joke I saw.*

But, the post drives home how important my next points will be to remember...

But that's my whole point is that you **can** find out so much knowledge, even the more obscure stuff, on the tens of billion or more websites that exist on the internet - if not more.

I'm certain that by the time I completed typing this chapter a few hundred more websites have started their internet existence.

And a few tens of thousands of websites by the time this book *is* written - if I were to look at this concept in terms of a flashback, in a way…

The more obscure sites, such as ones that may answer the above-mentioned funny 'asking for a friend', won't really lead to the knowledge useful for your next job.

But researching those sort of information <u>can</u> make you knowledgeable for writing stories, but also enrich your mind in more broader strokes.

You just need to become excellent in your critical reading and writing skills to do this.

You'll need to be able to distinguish 'fact' from 'fiction', 'truth' from 'a lie', 'things that didn't happen' from 'things that did happen.'

Fiction is about speculation for a part of a plot.

But to be good at using the skills on offer, you also *need* to become good at distinguishing which of the things you read, **are** facts.

The information on the internet won't make you smarter, or better equipped for a job if you don't use what you learn, especially not if you're reading or processing it in a critical way.

It can be fun stuff to know for story writing but if your goal is to get a good job you need to be able to distinguish the factual information that is useful from the information that is NOT.

Remember what I said about changing your mindset.

One part of this process is also to become more critical of the information around you.

In a way, I'd say my 'ex' pulled the wool over my eyes in terms of what he always told me.

An example of this is, when a few weeks after being told he's leaving me, to receive a phone call from his former boss - my 'ex' omitted to mention that he'd quit his job.

I'm not going into what the phone call was about but it wasn't that flattering in regards to how my 'ex' was described by his former boss, who actually felt sorry for me.

But this phone call was what made it more of a reality that things in my life were changing…

I guess that I'm more of a sceptic these days *because* of what happened on that day. I don't immediately believe what I'm told, what I read or what I see happen on the news.

You **can** be sceptical as well but you do your research to decide what is true *or* not.

When you treat the world in a new way with your new 'self' you can cause that new job to come from it.

From it, came my job as an author…

You can use this method to gain a job in your own chosen career. Facts can help you from being a person who gets caught up in the "long weight" and instead will walk away after just seconds.

If you're more sceptical about the information you will also be more critical of the sort of job you get and how you do this job.

In the end, you are in control of who you want to be and what way you want to appear to be to the world, and the new work colleagues, so always approach every with a critical mind.

"Being critical" in this context means that you scrutinise things. It doesn't mean you are mean to another person and say condescending remarks to them.

There are two different "being critical," and it's the version where it makes **you** capable of delivering constructive criticism you want to embrace…

This Page Left Intentionally Blank…
for you to write in.

Chapter Four:

Friendshipping

Introduction

While the healing process is ongoing you'll find yourself less inclined to be around friends. How do you deal with 'mutual friends' when a break-up happens? What do you say to anyone?

Personally, I lost the mutual friends. But it doesn't matter. Because, instead, I'm making friends who are solely **my** friends.

Any new friends won't really realise who my 'ex' is, and frankly, I don't really talk about him much, so it's unlikely that I'd accidentally end up with "mutual friends."

Friendships are important. Personally, I value each and every friendship I have, and often friendships are the beginning of better things.

For example, a friendship could lead to a new business venture. An example of this on an individual basis are the founders of Airbnb or Ben & Jerry's.

In the author world, as a similar example, an anthology of stories may come from a group of author friends getting together and deciding to do this as a joint venture.

Friends are important in other ways too. They are people you can talk to when you need an outlet. They're the people who lift you up when you feel down. They cheer you on when you make your latest claim to success - which can include them cheering you on as you find a new love.

This is kind of what happened to me when I met my new guy. Many of those who were there when my new guy and started our relationship were there when I announced that I was moving in with him... finally. It was the start of the best time of my life...

Value those who choose you as a friend. You earn friends by the way you treat people, in the way that you speak to them and by the kindness you demonstrate.

Trust is earned. So are friendships.

There are ways to start gaining a new circle of friends when you find yourself without the mutual friends you shared with an 'ex' and that's by meeting them in person or to do this online. Some people are not comfortable with new environments so the online option is better for you.

I'm introvert, even though I **will** voice myself strongly **if** I see someone being nasty to someone I consider a friend. (see more about this in the **Intro Going Outro** chapter)

Because, in the end, friendships are some of the most valuable commodities around, and the best relationships involving love should always start with friendship. Life is better when you have friends. It keeps you healthier **and** your mind active.

There are a few thoughts that often cross my mind:

- Should have tried to have many friends?
- How much effort do I need to put into a friendship?
- Is 'being friendly' a friendship?

The answer to these questions just depends on what your goal is. If you're happy with two or three friends that's perfectly okay. Just be friendly with everyone else. Even if you don't call someone a friend they may call you a friend in return.

In terms of effort, the biggest effort comes from treating people with kindness and showing a good character that people will appreciate.

And 'being friendly' IS a form of friendship TOO.

It's just not an intimate version of friendship where you might tell all your most personal information to the person. But it is a situation where the two of you have a rapport going on. It CAN lead to a closer friendship.

You can also be friends or be friendly with a work colleague, but you do need to be more careful there in case you end up leaving the job.

Why Letting Go Is Sometimes Better

Life before the breakup came with shared friends as a 'package deal'. Or so I thought. When the breakup came, it broke up friendships too. Those friends chose to stay friends with my ex-husband.

But I've been thinking about it ever since it happened and actually found it to be for the better. The words from my mother, who stated to me that things lost could be replaced by better things, well, I took her words to heart, and I decided to replace friends too.

If I was going to have friends it wasn't friends who would be the cause for a conflict of interest, who might "report back" anything I said, and who, ultimately, would tell my ex-husband about any new love I would meet.

Letting go is better in many ways. You create a clean break mentally, emotionally, financially, but why not *also* in terms of friends. You may not be able to do anything about family, especially if you have children, but friends are something to let go.

Besides, I find it deplorable that kids should suffer from losing touch with family members just because their parents ended up separating or divorcing.

My parents divorced when I was a teen and my siblings were *too* young to understand why they suddenly had no contact with the family. I never had any kids of my own but if I did have them I would have let them have contact with the family of my ex-husband.

But somehow, in the way he behaved with friendships, the idea wasn't mutual.

So letting go became the only option to go with for me.

It was the better option too because now I could determine in a more genuine way what values I cared about the most, and when I'd meet new people I could seek out friendships with people demonstrating those values.

My new guy, who started off as a friend, was one such individual.

You can write down on the blank page at the end of this chapter the five values you appreciate personally. Keep those in mind while you work on recovering from this break-up and as you rebuild the life that's ahead of you.

So you know, my values include honesty, trust, generosity, duty and loyalty.

Yes, it _may_ now strike you as ODD to read that honesty **is** a value I appreciate the most _because_ I wrote this book using an assumed pen name.

But, there's a difference between doing something to protect integrity (meaning with this that I don't want to be sued wrongfully by my 'ex' for the inclusion of examples of why my marriage had failed; also wouldn't want him to gain a chance to do a so-called 'kiss and tell' story) and being honest towards those around you.

Most of the people I know also know they can rely on me for confidentiality, trust that what they tell me won't become gossip and that they have a friend who won't abandon them when the going gets tough.

And the latter is founded in understanding loyalty as well having a duty of care to those around me.

Now for the opposite that can also happen, and which can become the reason for a marriage or other relationship to fail, and that's cheating. When a person cheats they betray their honesty and loyalty to the person they proclaimed their love towards; and the person they're supposed to be with, and it's something that did happen to me and I don't agree with such behaviour.

But before you start telling me that cheating has nothing to do with friendships, you are **right**. It has nothing to do with that. But such an experience CAN taint how you view friendships **later on** as you lose some of your trust in people.

Also, the other negative effect a failed relationship has comes in the loneliness it causes. You lose trust in people, and to lift yourself up from such loneliness can be a huge hurdle.

You will find yourself alone, and you will lack contact with others. Humans **are** social creatures.

Our whole society, from prehistoric day to the current time, is based around the idea that **we** want to live in societies and belong. This same society also would lead to conflicts over the same period and, in a way, friendship ending is conflict too.

Instead of dwelling on what you lost, it's better to let it go…

And YES, I **did** have to put that song from that movie in your head. I guess you'll be cursing me for the next few days as "Let It Go" circles in your mind endlessly.

Three lines from the song are quite powerful, and they have stuck with me ever since I saw the movie:

> *Don't let them in, don't let them see*
> *Be the good girl you always have to be*
> *Conceal, don't feel, don't let them know*

My interpretation of these few words is that it's expected for a person to weather the tough days. The end of the movie (a spoiler if you haven't seen it) is that it is 'love' that melts her sister from the ice prison, and sets things right between the sisters.

So, yes, let it go but don't shut the love or good feelings it can bring. As the title of this book says…heartbreak doesn't last forever.

After you've let go of the sadness, the anger, the pain, you need to rebuild the heart, fill the void with new memories, learn to trust again. It will take time but eventually, you will have moved on from this period of your life.

Remember **not** to assume that anyone new you meet will be like someone you had to let go…

Switching Off

By switching off I mean taking a break from social media, and the world in general. It can feel tough to deal with 'being social' when you feel down at the bottom of the barrel.

I went through a period myself, and actually, it was good that I didn't have internet at the time. It meant I could concentrate on myself rather than having to do things to meet expectations that people had. One of them was "Get over it already."

Yes, someone *did* actually tell me these words. I tell you to run a mile *if* any person ever suggests this because you don't need to get over 'it'.

Yes, I did say previously to 'let it go' but that's not the same as 'getting over it.'

Your emotions are a key part of who you are. What we perceive as negative emotions, most commonly the emotional response that is seen as a negative emotion is usually anger.

But in my opinion is that anger is an extreme version of the other negative emotion and that emotion is upset. Feeling upset, feeling like you want to cry **is** a release, and when you feel anger this is where the upset has gone to a maximum version of the upset.

When my 'ex' left I felt angry. However, deep down below this anger, there was also this extreme pain and it fuelled the anger. **MY anger...**

When emotion gets this painful this is when you need to switch off from the world. No, you want to ignore the world around you. You just switch off and take time off from being around the world.

How you unload this anger is important though. Let me give a comparison to something else that people do to an extreme at times.

People get drunk. And when you're drunk you will wake up with a hangover and a massive headache or similar symptoms (or so I've always been told - I don't drink so I don't know).

When you get angry that's like being stone drunk, being so drunk that you'd pass out. And then when you wake up with the hangover you're going from this extreme to your normal self.

When you get angry you reach an extreme in your emotion, and you need to give yourself time to cool off before you interact with people. This is why it's always advised to walk away and give yourself ten minutes before you send an email you've written while angry.

Or you receive a letter that makes you angry wait ten minutes before calling the sender.

If all this sounds familiar then it is because if you're a parent (or watching parenting programmes on television) you will know about the "time-out method" for children. It suggests one minute of 'time-out' for every year a child's age is, so if a child is five years old you give such a child five minutes of time-out.

Marriage, especially when you have problems in it (and I did during mine) is also a place where a similar action **can** be applied.

If your husband, wife, boyfriend, girlfriend reacts angrily to YOU then, applying the *above* time-out is actually handy (yes, it **DID** work for me), and you **can** give each year of your marriage together a minute of time BEFORE responding towards the angry person.

You give yourself the time to come up with a calm, considered response BUT also give the other person the chance to calm down. This rule applies to both people!

It's actually hilarious to think back that my 'ex' didn't realise I was using a "time-out method" designed for unruly children as a way to punish them for misbehaviour to give <u>him and the real "me"</u> a time-out...

Okay, most of the time he **did** stay angry, accusing me of not wanting to answer his questions though, often, he was unhinged in the way he behaved, especially towards the end of the marriage.

But the enforced time-out **did** have a good effect on **me**.

I started to realise I didn't like **any** type of conflict or argument.

It caused me to start to "switch off" and this lead to the idea that switching off was **good** for me.

Switching off is like that vitamin B, orange juice and plenty of water one should drink (thank a biker for this suggestion he'd mentioned when my 'ex' was drunk at one point), because consuming these will essentially reset your body from the effects of being drunk.

Similarly, a time-out resets your mood and emotions from feeling an extreme emotion such as anger to a more neutral emotion.

If you are in a failing relationship right now or have a friendship that seems to be fizzling out, then I suggest doing a time-out.

In the relationship, give each other space by doing your own thing. In a friendship just give each of you some time away from the friendship. In both cases, if it's not meant to be there will be a break-up or loss and that also means this book will help you in other ways.

'Switching off' **is** good for your mood, mind, emotions, and your overall health. It's an action where **you** reset these aspects of your being. You can do this multiple times throughout your life.

You can do this after a job is lost, when a relationship ends, after bereavement, and more.

So, the next time someone you know, on social media, says something along the lines of "I think I'm switching off from being on social media for a few days/weeks/months" you should wish them well and tell them to take as much time as needed…

Be FRIENDS with yourself

When you're starting over with life after a break-up there are **many** things you need to change in your life, however, the first thing to do is to start being friends with yourself once more. Because I'm certain you'll feel like everything is lost to you, and you can't go on.

"But I will tell you that you can go on and you WILL."

These were the *first* words of encouragement I'd been given *after* I was finally alone *after* my 'ex' had left me for good…

I decided this was a good idea, and using **Journaling**, I'd work out how to be friends with **myself**.

I continue this process to this day, mostly to reaffirm the realisation I had discovered.

Being friends with yourself is the **only** friendship in your life you CAN be in control of.

It's a unique sort of friendship and, barring the suggestion that it is making you almost guilty of talking to yourself (*everyone* should have heard the comical suggestion that "talking yourself is the first sign of madness"), however, in this case, you're probably the <u>sanest</u> you can ever be!

Now how **do** you become friends with yourself?

In part, the answer lies in the process of changing your mindset. Include in this the idea that learning to be friends with yourself involves **also** a change in your mindset.

Don't assume that, somehow, you were never friends with yourself.

Instead, I'm going to suggest that you simply forgot how to be friends with yourself. Because when you're in a bad relationship this is easy to do, and I've always felt there is a direct link between being self-confident and feeling a sense of loving oneself thus being friends with yourself.

Once you were a child with hopes and dreams and you wanted to be someone growing up.

So was I.

When the days of happiness turned into more and more days of sorrow and emotional pain I wondered more often daily if I could ever be happy again, or whether things would change to the days of happiness I had experienced before.

It would be reminded to me that I could be friends with myself once my 'ex' had left, and at the same time I was also told: "Before you can love someone new you need to love yourself first once more."

It took effort and a bucket load of willpower but I DID do what this person told me.

I know YOU can do the same.

The reason why I started telling to change your mindset and not with the topic of friendship is precisely this.

By changing your mindset you're becoming friends with yourself once more, and possibly with a stronger and more confident version of yourself.

Now obviously *your* next question is going to be this one: "How do I tell people I'm doing this process of change in me?"

Easy.

You don't tell. You SHOW.

You may have heard these words before in the context of book writing before, and it was when I started to write stories I realised that these words not only apply to how a book presents itself but also in how you can make certain people can see that you change as a person. Oftentimes, in a story, it states that from the first to the last page of a book a character has to have grown in their outlook on life, in their characterisation, and has to have matured.

Now, do you see why I'm presenting this book more like a story about how I changed my life after a divorce (show!) instead of doing endless lists of "do this and then this and then this" (tell). It's better to show a person how change helped and for such a person to adapt it to themselves than to tell them to change and for such a person to try and figure out how…

As I said before in the subchapter 'How can I change how I behave?' there will always be doubters who will suggest to you (or others) that you cannot or won't change.

My suggestion, repeatedly now, is never to listen to them or to believe them.

Believe in yourself.

Believe in the changes you are creating in your life.

Then become your own best friend.

In the chapter **Intro Going Outro** I'll tell you about how I handled all this WHILE *also* living with depression and having anxiety.

Because, despite what you may believe, it can happen even if you have depression and/or anxiety. If you take on this process without doubting in yourself (although from time to time you may feel in that way), you can not only change BUT also have a positive impact making **each** of these conditions less prominent and less debilitating.

New Friends, New Beginnings

A day will come when you start meeting new people, and after that, you will make a friend, and then another one. I would take your time with this though. Friendships need to be fostered **slowly** because you need to learn to trust people once more.

Trust is **definitely** earned. You need to set boundaries in terms of any new friends.

One boundary is to tell them you need time to recover from your break-up, or if this is a case that you lost a friend you'd trusted and respected for ANY reason, you can also ask that you become friends slower.

You don't become a best friend with someone in a day.

But if you work on it as a longterm goal you will be called "friend" eventually.

There's likely something you shared that caused you to feel

like you had a common bond. It will be hard to build that same bond with someone else, especially when such a person already has their own friends.

But it's your behaviour which will make **you** welcome as "the new friend" and earns you more of the group as a friend.

It's this reason why I say that you're not just befriending "a person" but instead become friends with an individual **and** their whole circle of friends at the **same** time. Treat those *other* friends with respect, and they'll start to accept you, and ultimately you could end up with several friends.

As I said in the Introduction of this chapter 'being friendly' is a form of friendship, **too**. I'm a believer in this concept of being friendly with as many people as you can, **but** to be strong friends with a few of them closely.

Strangely enough, it's been something I've believed in since early childhood despite going through a difficult childhood and despite having a big dent put into that belief by the events involving my less than rosy marriage and the messy divorce that followed.

A new beginning in a new place can benefit you greatly. It will wipe the slate clean in terms of memories associated with the place they were created.

A new place can bring with it, new friends. It can help you re-evaluate what you want from life.

Friendships come and go.

I know that.

However, treat each of them as relevant to **when** it existed.

Learn from each friendship the things you want. Like everything else you learn from in life, this is also a valuable tool to become a better person.

New friends teach you new values, new ways of doing things, and new behaviours.

New friends can also restore your sense of belonging.

They can heal the wounds left behind whenever you lose another friend or if you've ended a relationship with an ex.

There is **no** limit (EVER!) as to how a friend will affect you and you should always hope that they treat you with kindness, respect and someone you should be able to trust. You're in control of how you treat them though, and this is the values you should bring to a friendship.

Besides going out into social settings (pub, cafe, clubs) there's another place and way to find these new friends, and that's by doing arts or crafts and this may be a welcome alternative to going social in the other options listed here.

This Page Left Intentionally Blank…
for you to write in.

Chapter Five:

Go Creative

Introduction

Creativity doesn't come naturally to everyone. I understand it. But being creative is something you can do just for YOU.

No one needs to see the drawings or other art (or the crafted things) you create. But there's one thing you **will** be able to be certain of. If you keep practising you **can** become better at it. And if you DO want people to see what you create, you'll gain confidence in other parts of your life from doing so.

There's often an idea that creativity allows people to be critical, but remember that those people who are giving criticism may not even be able to do the same as you are doing.

Okay, I'll admit it. I can't sing to save my life. When I'm alone I'll belt out alongside my favourite songs and just butcher them to pieces. Do I care about how well I sing…or not? Of course not. I do it because it's fun for ME and it's so I can have an outlet.

Doing crafts or drawing has something therapeutic to it that can really zone you out.

Crafts and drawing is probably the number one therapy treatment that exists and that everyone should do regardless of whether he or she has life problems on his or her plate.

Yes, even drawing stick people IS art. Singing out of tune is singing. Writing a crappy story is still writing. EVERYTHING that you keep doing is something that enriches your skills and makes you better…

Yes, even cutting weirdly shaped pieces of newspaper and then arranging them into strange creatures with glue IS crafting.

There is NO bad art. There is NO useless crafting.

Get a few lumps of Sculpey and make this crafting material into many different weird creatures. The crazier and the more colourful it becomes the more fun it will make it for you.

BECAUSE the more you do something the better you get at it.

If like me, you write often, you get better at it. If like me, you do digital art often, you get better at it. Hmm, but that singing. Nope, not going to get better, although I'm watching YouTube videos from singers about breathing exercises so perhaps I DO get better at using my lungs in the end. There's auto-tune for "singers" such as I. Okay, enough about this singing…

I have started being fascinated about doing watercolour. I last did this years ago (before I was married to be precise). I may be out of practice but if I do it I will relearn, and if I keep doing it I will get better at it.

This principle applies to everything you do.

If you dance a lot you do it better.

If you cook a lot you do it better.

If you work on relationships you do them better. All of them. Even if it takes time to see the end result of them.

So, embrace your potential creativity and get it going. Have fun…

Art As Therapy

Art is a **perfect** way for you to relax, and to find that stillness **we** all want from life from time to time.

Art has been with humans as a way to express ourselves for many thousands of years to communicate spirituality, to be a way to communicate with whatever higher beings the ancient humans believed in, whether doing it or appreciating it.

I know not everyone is a perfect artist, but don't worry about whether you are drawing that nose correctly, or whether your person resembles a stick person more. Play with colours and blending them because there's something nice that comes from that too. I bet you'd have a smile on your face doing that.

And I shouldn't forget the finger painting. If your kids are young then I encourage you and them all sit down and make this a family activity. Because you don't realise it perhaps but THEY need to heal too if their parents have split up.

So, art is a therapy that heals wounds, that brings the remaining family closer (even if it's for a while), and the synapses it forms in your mind while doing it have been shown to do a lot of healing of the mind, body and spirit.

The colours of nature are so plentiful and if you can't bring yourself to start with the paint brushes or pencils, you can perhaps do photography. Remember that your goal is to capture the colour in nature so don't try to do the most perfect photos.

I stated in the Introduction for this chapter that the more you something the better you get at it.

To give you an example about myself. I can't knit. But I want to start to learn it so I can knit my own clothing which means I can knit myself a big chunky knitted garment to keep warm in the winter without worrying about what size guides a shop might be using, and so I can knit it in the colours I like.

Doing crafts is a form of art too.

Instead of saying "I can't do this" I say instead "I can't do this yet."

Adding the word **YET** to sentences is a very important way of self-validation. Read the following sentences (all relate to things I've done over the last decade or so) with the word YET added to them (obviously not included to demonstrate what I mean).

"I can't do web design______"

"I can't knit______"

"I can't speak a new language______"

"I can't walk for a long distance______"

Write in the word YET at the end of each sentence with a red pen and now look at it again and see how different self-validation makes something.

Because you're now saying that something you don't know how to do is something you don't YET it suddenly makes you realise that, perhaps, there's a chance to learn.

"I don't how to be a successful author______"

This is the latest self-validation I'm working on. In my own mind the wording is already changing to the following:

"I know how to be a successful author."

Except for the knitting and the language, all the self-validation is happening. And these are just a few of the hundred or so ideas I wrote down in my notebook while doing Journaling.

On the blank page at the end of the chapter write five important things you want to learn to do and which, obviously, you haven't learned **yet**. I'm not suggesting that learning involves getting yourself a degree, but if you DO have such a dream start working on it.

One of most inspiring stories I heard about in 2017 is of a lady becoming a voice actor for the game World of Warcraft with her "A Turtle Made It To The Water" and the in-game character who says this Scrollsage Nola.

The quest she gives involves you saving a number of baby turtles from albatrosses and crabs. If you search the voice actor Maryann Strossner on the website wowpedia.com you'd read she is 93 years old. In the World of Warcraft gaming community, she's become everyone's grandma…

But it's a story such as this that teaches us that we're never too old to learn something new, that we're **never** too old to start something new - I was in my late forties when I started writing, or **never** too old to start afresh in life INCLUDING starting a new love life if you so wished.

So, rather than saying "I can't___," say instead "I haven't yet___", and do this for **everything** you don't know how to do. In terms of art, you haven't yet done something and that something will make you feel so much better.

Ms Strossner, when asked, said that was convinced she could do it (the voice acting that is) and set out to do it. So just buy yourself paper, a few pencils and colouring pencils and draw. If you so wish you will always be the only one to see the work.

I'll talk in the next chapter how to take that next step to go from doing this activity on your own to doing it with others.

And the latter is a big step when you are also dealing with anxiety but there are other ways to be less alone that don't involve being around others if it makes you uncomfortable…

Creativity Is A Cure For Loneliness

You don't need to do arts and crafts alone. An art school (or similar) can be a good place to get new friends, as stated in the subchapter **New Friends, New Beginnings**.

Also, remember when you start doing a new activity of any kind that you don't need to be friends with the people overnight at the art school or other places where you go to learn new skills. Share a common interest first with them.

Be brave with your skill. You don't become a skilled artist or craft person overnight.

Yes, the **same** suggestion I made relating to friendships also applies to creativity.

You can learn to be creative!

Art, crafts, writing, photography, cooking, a degree studied, and many others are a route towards a more creative mind.

A creative mind needs nourishing and once you've learned any skill the easiest and best way to keep the knowledge fresh is to learn more.

Not just from books or web pages, but also from people.

People around you offer an endless wealth of information, skill and horizons…and the chance to gain many new friends IF you go with my aforementioned idea that "being friendly" **is** its own form of friendship.

Sharing knowledge is like the nerve fibres or axons that connect everything in our own bodies.

You *may* have heard the term "six degrees of separation," which is an idea where everyone and everything is **six or fewer steps** away from each other.

A friend of a friend *may* be the person who gets you the information to start a new job.

Or they could be the person who introduces *you* to someone who'd become the new love in your life.

Even something as ambiguous as "playing a computer game" requires a fair amount of creativity. I stated before I met my new guy playing an online game.

One might think that playing a game such as this is a waste of time, however, there was a psychologist back in 2010 (if I remember the year correctly) who suggested that one should be looking differently at online games and hobbies.

She argued that gaming and doing hobbies, in general, offer a method for a person to learn skills that *can* help in the work environment. She suggested they give a person the skill of being resourceful.

Okay, that's just the "too long; didn't read" version of what she said.

Here's what I recall of what she did say in relation to online gaming (the text is my "not verbatim" interpretation of it, that is, how I applied her statement to make myself more creative and more capable of being able to interact with others despite being an introvert).

It will allow you to become better at communicating intent towards others especially if you are doing "raids" which are organised group events with ten or more people.

You have what's know as "professions" and to level them up and then use them to earn an income you need to plan how to get the materials for to make things, or how to earn the gold to buy items needed. You cannot be playing 24/7 so you need to learn to manage the time you do have with precision thus allowing you to become good at time management.

Communication should include attempts at being polite, friendly and kind, which are traits you want for a job. If you haven't had a job, explain skills in terms of what it entails to be a "raid leader", putting the emphasis on the leadership part, on what you achieved (levelling a character to maximum with minimal time spent playing the game and being able to be a successful entrepreneur by doing a lot of selling on the auction house…

Yes, I know it may not land you a job saying this, but according to the psychologist who spoke about the positive side of playing a game it will contribute towards creating a creative, productive and resourceful mindset that can say "I can do this."

Similarly, if you do a hobby you're planning the use of materials to maximise the output from them, and even here you'll be working on such things as time management and being resourceful.

The bonus here is that you can put the <u>end-product</u> on Etsy, or similar sites, and sell them and turn the hobby into a thriving business.

Similar applies to a writing career.

With practice, you would obviously become a **better** writer, and then the moment comes when **you** want to sell books… I say to you "GO FOR IT" if that's your wish.

Creativity When...?

When you have **other** things on your mind it's probably hard to start doing art or crafts. But it's something you **want** to be doing, regardless of whatever else is on your mind.

Because this is the <u>perfect</u> time for you to contemplate over what happened before and to do the necessary soul-searching.

The time spent on arts or crafts (or both), on writing, on any form of pastime really, is that part of the day you should make into **"me time."**

It all depends on how much time you have available.

I'm fully aware this book will be read by many busy parents with young children. When you're in this kind of situation, especially when you've been left alone with them after a divorce, you need to put their needs first of course. But remember that your future plans affect them so creating a business out of your own creativity can help them in the long run...

So I suggest that you want to figure out how to **maximise** what you can get out every ounce of spare time you have available, but at the same time never to assume that ANY time spent on anything you do is wasted time.

I think that the cell phone is the best tool ever invented for a busy life.

So with a notepad and a pen plus a cell phone at hand, you have the means to do a lot of your planning, organising and putting ideas to paper "on the go."

Have an idea, pull out that cell phone, run an app to record you saying your idea. You can even dictate a book in this way as I know authors who do this.

I have friends, who are writers like I am, and who often tell on their social media feed that they do their writing of books by getting up a half hour earlier *before* their kids are awake.

If that's one way to create this "me time" then go for it.

Also, I'm using writing as an example here as it's what I do as a career and it's easier to use something familiar as an example to illustrate an idea…

Remember that "me time" IS NOT ever selfish!!!

By creating "me time" you're actually taking care of the mind. In the first two chapters, I suggested you need to nurture and also soothe your mind.

This "me time" is precisely why you want such time available.

I'll go into more detail of why "me time" is **so** important when I discuss the benefits of **Journaling** in the next subchapter.

"When…?"

Yes, it was one of the first questions I voiced looking at my life to date.

I felt at first that somehow I had to justify or even validate a reason to be creative. You see, the reason why that was the case is *that* I'd lived for a decade in the environment of my broken marriage where every other day I might possibly hear from my 'ex': "You're worthless…" (or similar sentiment).

I think it's this reason why it took me six years before I even felt the courage to start writing stories in the first place.

I guess you will have similar feelings right now about your life after the divorce.

When I changed the narrative to "You have worth" is when I started to realise I could be creative AND use the creativity in a positive way. One of the byproducts of that sentiment resulted in this book where I tell the story of how I changed my mindset from a fatalistic view of failure and despair to one where I could start over and be the better person.

No, this sentiment has nothing to do with "trying to win" in comparison to whatever my 'ex' may be doing. Frankly said, I have NO interest in knowing what he's doing and this is why I purposefully blocked him on social media in as many places as possible.

My 'ex' may think I did this to compete, but as I was reminded when I first started writing stories: *"Write for yourself, because if you do that you're writing with your heart and mind, and not to seek validation or approval in the eyes of any other person. Write what you believe and your authenticity will shine."*

YOUR authenticity will shine **too** when you give yourself "me time."

Your voice as a genuine individual is discovered and it evolves during this "me time." One other reason why you need to give yourself time to heal after a break-up as you do give up some of your voice during a relationship of any kind, and even in a relationship that's perfect and happy you do this.

So, even if you are happily married and reading this book out of curiosity, give yourself permission to create some "me time."

Never ever let it come to "When...?" because there's never a better time than RIGHT NOW.

Journaling

I've only done some journaling myself, however, I know of individuals who do it **often**, though I sometimes think that I should do it more because they tell me it's a way for us to unload whatever is on our mind onto the paper inside a notebook.

At its core, it's an activity that helps with managing stress. Instead of bottling up the associated emotions you put it on paper.

In a way, the content of this book was "journaled" because, as you may notice, it's more a collection of thoughts rather than being a book about self-help.

But most of the best books to help with emotion, stress or similar topic that I've always read are those that go to the process of thinking about the issue rather than trying to dictate a "this is how to do it."

By journaling, you do the process for yourself.

Instead of forcing you into an abrupt action you guide your emotions away from what caused the stress and towards the relief of the stress.

"It helps me process the feelings after I had lost my father…"

That's the comment from a prolific journaling practitioner I know of on YouTube.

She said it allowed her to move on, process the pain, and to start afresh. (I cannot include this individual's name for privacy reasons by the way). But she has taught me that journaling is good.

For *me*, art is my journaling.

When I need stress relief I'll doodle…

From me, doing all this doodling came my new desire to do beautiful graphics on my computer, and because of *that*, I got into designing my own book covers.

And yes, I'm remembering my own words that the more you do something the better you get at it. To date, the real "me" has done perhaps a hundred nice, and not so nice, book cover ideas (some will be on future books I publish).

Such is the stress relief I get from doing art that I decided to do that for a few hours and design a book cover for a story I want to write in my real identity, and afterwards, for me at least, it unblocked the flow of words to paper, thus speeding up the writing of *this* book.

If you can find a common theme for your journaling it can **be** fun and rewarding. It can increase your creative flair, and at the same time help you learn to do things in a different way, such as, for example, becoming more organised.

There are known benefits for doing journaling as an activity. It can help with:

- Managing anxiety.
- Stress reduction.
- Make it easier to manage depression.
- You can learn to prioritise problems and fears, and organise them.
- Unload thought, previously this would be done as a diary, and journaling and keeping a diary can be done alongside one another.
- You can make this a moment when you totally relax and even meditate.

However, also remember to live healthily, so check out the **Foodies 'n Nutrition** chapter for information to positively impact your health in additional ways.

If you do plan to do journaling, make it a daily activity, encourage yourself to write (or draw) every day). It can be done for a few minutes or a few hours, whichever feels better for you.

Make it easy. Keep a notebook in your reach with a pen to write down a thought - the blank pages in this book are a way for you get comfortable doing this, and also feel free to go overboard with annotating this book to pieces.

You can write down whatever you want in the notebook used for journaling. It's a private domain and no one ever needs to see it.

If you do this activity on a daily basis at the same time it will put some order into your chaotic life which will have long-term benefits.

This Page Left Intentionally Blank…
for you to write in.

Chapter Six:

Family vs Family

Introduction

When two people split up their immediate family also splits up. This may be different from family to family, but generally speaking, you'll find that the family will also split. Perhaps a few of the opposite family stay in touch, but not always, and not many of them.

It's okay if you lose touch with those family because ending a marriage also means you're not really family with them unless you have children.

And both for yourself and your children you need to choose whether to keep in touch.

Ask your children, if there are any, if they want to stay in touch with the family members of the person you were married to or a relationship with - it doesn't really matter whether you're straight or LGB because if children are involved they shouldn't be ignored or forgotten.

They will hurt just you do when your relationship with their other parent ends.

Not in the same way as you will hurt, but they **will** hurt.

It shouldn't be like this really with a situation of people going up against one another, but as the saying goes… "you can choose your friends but not your family".

Unfortunately, you will find people in the opposite family who will use this idea presented here to stop having contact with you and even any children.

Your children *may* experience the brunt of this *when* they suddenly don't have an aunt, uncle or grandparent.

All because the relationship between you and a spouse (or boyfriend or girlfriend) has ended.

Children shouldn't have to choose between parents either. It's unfair to them, and they may even feel like somehow *they* were to blame for what happened between you.

Not true, but their mind, which is less capable of reasoning and rationalising than that of an adult, will assume it is.

They may also end up blaming the absent parent for things if something isn't going well as a consequence of the separation of the family unit.

Decide on **who** you got on well of the opposite family, and if you can broach the subject of 'keeping in touch' via a letter or an email. If they say no, just say as a response that you will be there if ever they change their mind and leave it at that.

If there's animosity caused by your former spouse (or boyfriend or girlfriend) that would prevent this then just reach out with a simple "I know things didn't work out with him/her and myself but if you want to keep in touch feel free to do so."

IF a person says YES to keeping in touch, do explain in a calm, measured way that now that you're on your own you would like them to abide by behaviours you grew up with. They'll likely ask what these are. Make certain that trust and respect of personal space are two of the behaviours you communicate.

In the next chapter, I'm going into how I dealt with this sort of situations myself.

Listen to them...

occasionally!

When you communicate your wishes to former family members you have to be tactful, even cautious. In my case, I decided to sever all contact with them because, deep down, I knew that anything said to them would be told to my 'ex' and he'd use this against me in one fashion or another.

When something like that might happen, and it's highly likely if the split up wasn't amicable, then the best course of action IS to let go (as stated in a previous subchapter).

Walking away shows that you are the "grown-up" in the room, and I don't say this to be condescending.

As you **DO** *need* two people to have an argument it's this moment, when you walk away it's when the anger, frustration, possible lies or spite won't have an outlet... at least NOT FOR

YOU!!!

Remember that if the OTHER person started being angry about something silly, stupid or you, that you're not at fault of that behaviour and therefore you have no reason to have to explain yourself OR to apologise.

Do, however, make certain you accept their apology as doing so **stops** them having a reason to keep bringing up the situation later on.

Yes, I find conflict generally confusing and personally I wish that everyone just go on with one another…

To give you a simple example of this suggestion is to use 'watching television' as a comparison.

How scary is a horror movie **if** you have the sound turned off. **Try it**… I can assure you it **will** almost feel like a few minutes that are awkward in how laughable they are; almost like you're watching a comedy of sorts.

My opinion of 'walking away' so no argument can ensue is similar to what I suggest for a horror movie. Just be careful though as some situations will give the other person the feeling of aggravation. In a situation where there was a not so amicable split-up, the person could see the act of walking away as a reason to increase their behaviour.

A **better** way to do this is to have the phone switched off for a part of the day - another way to reclaim so "me time" as discussed earlier. When you're asked why you did this, don't give excuses.

Just make clear that "part of the day is 'me time' and you **want** the quiet of no contact with anyone." It's no excuse to want time for yourself.

Listening to the family **can** be beneficial as long as they also will listen to you as well.

Find a middle ground between what they want and what you want BUT always put your own needs first, and no, doing that doesn't make you selfish.

If you're not capable of taking care for your own needs **first**, you're going to stay stuck in the loop that made you *less* your own person in a relationship where the relationship ended up skewed in favour of the *other* person.

A good relationship is built on the idea of teamwork; it's supposed to be a partnership which is why my new guy and I always refer to one another as partners.

Because, at the core of it, we view what we have as a team, a partnership, a relationship of equals.

That's the sort of relationship **you** should strive to have with any person around you.

And if it **isn't** this sort of relationship then **don't** feel bad about walking away from it.

If it doesn't start off as a partnership it may grow in one but if the earliest signs show an unequal situation that fuels arguments that's a sign that things may get worse rather than better.

Yes, even walk away from contact with family members *if* being in contact with them causes you to feel less good about yourself, and certainly walk away from the ex-spouse's family if they listen to the viewpoints of your ex without giving your viewpoint a chance.

The idea that you can choose friends, but not family, is a bit **stupid** if you go down to the core of the ideas surrounding these words. In my opinion at least. Because you can choose the family too. Being related to them doesn't mean you need to have them in your life as dead weight, especially if there are conflicts in values.

It goes back to the idea of 'being friendly' as stated before. You don't need to be in contact constantly with the family who you may not agree with or even like. I have to grapple this all the time.

I have my occasional disagreements with family members from time to time, and when I interact with them, under those circumstances, I'll just take the approach of being friendly with them. I can't change their minds, which I don't like, but I decided to live with it. So, I work on adapting my behaviour, and I'll go into a mode of being friendly with them.

Listen, adapt and still do your own thing. That's the way forward…

Don't Take Their Side

If a situation arises when someone in your family splits up then the **better** option is to be neutral in your standing with both sides involved.

Taking a side in **any** conflict only will cause you to have issues with one *or* both of the individuals.

It can even cause conflict between yourself and the individuals involved.

In a way, this is what happened to me in regard to my former in-laws. Of course, they'd side with their son, but in doing so they forgot to ask me if what they were told was actually factual. I decided to walk away because that way I could show them that the conflict was purely caused by the behaviour of the person they decided to listen to.

To this day I don't know what their view is of the divorce and now I don't really care to know it any more...

The people who are splitting up are in enough pain without having to deal with *you* getting involved in what they're dealing with, and often the "being helpful" will be received less favourable.

When you see your family members getting involved in your split-up you can just ask them to just step back, and not be involved.

You can let them know that it's more helpful for you to get the advice or guidance from a neutral individual such as a lawyer, a marriage counsellor or perhaps a pastor at a church *if* you and your soon-to-be-ex-spouse are religious.

The idea of "taking sides" takes on *many* flavours throughout life. One of them is when a relationship ends, but let me start at the beginning…

The earliest version of a conflict, or "taking sides", that a person might encounter is the awkward situation of being bullied *or* being the bully in school.

This also, in my opinion, is the first place where children can be taught **not** to get into the behaviour of being a bully, and where someone tries to bully them for them **not** to react to the bullying.

A person, who was bullied at an earlier part of their life, might have brought this as 'luggage' into a future relationship *because* of insecurities about those around them.

Not always, but most people I've encountered throughout my life say, if bullied, they have left-over issues from such experiences.

The opposite is true, too, for the person who bullies, who *may* not see it as wrong to keep behaving in such a way throughout life. But even this can be different from person to person.

Although, in my personal life of the real "me" I've met people who showed **regret** *for being bullies earlier in their lives. Yes, these are the good sort of people that also can exist, who change how they behave and regret stuff they did as wrongdoing.*

For me, the contrast between this person and how my 'ex' still behaves is stark. My 'ex' never seems to have changed how he acted from the way he behaved during the marriage if I compare it to how he acted in the last (and probably final) time I'll ever see him my lifetime…

Taking sides can also be an aspect of 'being competitive'.

The above suggestion of certain people wanting to bully is a negative form of being competitive, and it was actually rather amazing to see someone be different from their former self 'as the bully.'

The more positive version of being competitive, in my opinion, is based around 'being cooperative' and 'learning to accept that things are often a challenge.'

In fact, your **whole** life can be one challenge after another.

Some people take such challenges in their stride while others struggle with these challenges.

I'm one of those who struggles with challenges, to be honest, so for me, the idea of getting supposedly "helpful being" was not actually helping me in the slightest for the most part. There were maybe one or two things that were helpful, but most of it didn't help.

So taking sides can have its consequences as shown by this bit of anecdotal reminiscing about the topic of bullying that actually is a "hot topic" in the news at the time of writing.

At the core of it, it involves people taking sides.

So now you see how easily it is to fall into such a pattern it may be easier to see why not getting involves is better.

However, that said, in situations where a person is being bullied it is better to tell a bully to STOP in such behaviour.

Let the person going through the situation **know** that you can help if needed.

That's the better approach to take, also, when a relationship ends.

Only offer to '**be there**' for the individuals involved without getting involved directly and definitely without taking any side in the matter, regardless of whether the person is your direct family member, or whether it's the 'other person.'

Near the end, when there's a conflict the two people having the conflict can figure out how to move forward, and whether the conflict remains or is resolved. But the purpose of this book is how to cope when conflict isn't resolved and you have a broken heart from it.

Learn from what happened. Make certain you change and are not the same person the other person knew. I'll go into more of this process of how I view it and dealt with it in terms of the family in the next subchapter…

Be Your Own Individual

Within your family you were able to establish an identity of your own as you were growing up as a child; when you were becoming an adult; when you started on the path to establishing a relationship with someone you want to spend the rest of your life with…

Having an identity is what defines us as individuals within our society of more than seven billion individuals, all with their own hopes, dreams, customs and traditions.

The drive to be recognised as an individual has a long path in human history, and that path comes with many bumps and potholes in it really…

From the earliest 'hunter-gatherer', who worked *for* the group of tribesmen and tribeswomen they belonged in, to the computer programmer, who works for their own purpose, the history in between has been long and filled with **many** challenges to allow the *individual* to be(come) their *own* person.

Some people in current time *assume* that an individual isn't allowed to be an individual, while others strive do devalue what makes each of us an individual in our own right.

Laws were invented to allow for these changes to happen, and laws keep changing to allow for this change to happen more and more. Laws are designed to make certain that certain types of individualism are shown to be wrong, while other laws strive to embellish the positive aspects of certain behaviours, such as, for example: *"I have a dream…"*

Religion shaped over time to allow individual choice in what to believe (or not to believe). Everything I said above about laws applies to religion as well in a way.

Economic systems evolved, and became specialised in certain cases, to allow for a drive for commerce to happen or to curtail its progress. No ideal economic system has yet been created by humans to make everyone happy.

The sum of history, both that of your personal family and of the wider community, led to where you found yourself as you were growing up.

There's a marked difference between an individual growing up in an affluent family or one where family members worked in a kitchen, mine or as a day labourer (I based this viewpoint on discussions with different individuals and listening to what was said and how the person has reacted to the information).

All of these experiences within the family are told about and defined who you became.

But, you're your own individual.

Even though you're shaped by your environment, your family history and society as a whole, you should always shape your own views, and form your own critical thinking about how your existence in the world.

When you start a relationship you'll encounter a **new** set of values and views.

Both from the new partner as well as a new group of individuals who have the potential to become family (remember what I said before about "you can choose your friends but not your family" as well as "be friendly" with what I'm talking about now).

This analogy *also* applies to friendships to a degree which is a whole other…

Different families have **different** concepts for the idea of being your own individual.

A family where *someone* became this successful business owner **will** have a different idea of individualism than a family where someone tries to do the same and fails in doing achieving such success.

In one family, individualism will be associated with success; in the other family, individualism will be viewed as the cause of failure.

It will have formed the values within a family. So, if you come from a family where individualism is valued, it **may** cause issues if you get together with someone who is brought up to be against this. Again, this is sometimes, but **not** all the time.

Yes, you guessed it right if you started to think: "Did N. Lee get into a relationship with someone who didn't value individualism?"

The answer is: "YES."

My family was one where individualism was encouraged, or at least I feel that was the situation. I grew up with hearing a story about my great-grandmother running a hotel. She owned it, managed it, she was "boss" to the staff there. It created the idea of "wanting to own a business of my own" in me.

This idea of me wanting to own and to run a business, was frowned on by 'ex' who saw *any* attempt on my part to start a business as competition to his own attempts to start a business. Rather than doing this as a joint effort, he wanted to do it all *himself*, and in doing so, he *forgot* I wanted the same.

Remember where I stated that *N.Lee* is an alias to **prevent** my 'ex' from doing a lawsuit for the <u>imagined</u> criticisms of him in this book…

…My real *"me"* is running a business now, and my real *"me"* is working on creating a business with **my new guy**. (insert super happy smiley face here!)

My new guy, unlike my 'ex', encourages me in my pursuit to be a business owner.

He was brought up with the sense of individualism = successful in a career AND success in pursuit of running a business.

Once the business is created my new guy **won't** frown on my efforts; instead, he's encouraging me to keep going and to work on succeeding with it.

Notice the contrast between my life with my 'ex' and my current life with my new guy.

This is also, ironically, an illustration of how **different** the values between two different families can be.

So, in your pursuit of being who **you** want to be you need to be considerate of family, and friends *too*.

However, while this is going on, never allow yourself to be changed from who you want to be, and instead always work on adapting yourself to fit in with the "expected moulds" people present towards you.

Because I'm an individualistic person at my core I do everything to "go with the flow." The part of me that doesn't like conflict helps in making this a smooth process.

And, secretly, I work on changing *their* hearts and *their* minds to think more as I do. Or so I hope…

People don't often notice it when they're influenced in a positive way, and in the end, just tend to think it's their own minds that changed them.

Which is actually **good** because when positive change comes from one's **own** mind it tends to stick…

In a way, this is correct because there's a high value in "lead by example."

A person who's *less* inclined to seek out conflict influences people around them to be *less* inclined to seek it out either.

So being your own individual, especially with the bonus features of showing how to trust, how to be kind and caring, being understanding, etc comes with the perk of being who you want to **BE**!

So, all in all, if you find yourself at the end of a road because a relationship ends, make this the time to re-assess your own individual characteristics using the information from the first two chapters for this process.

Life is a lifelong learning process of adapting, adjusting and re-evaluating. I do these things on a daily basis, even though and BECAUSE I'm in a good relationship with my new guy.

I guess his opinion of being in love with "his best friend" says I'm doing something right.

So, find that **perfect** equilibrium for yourself between being a person in your own right, and being acceptable to those around you, and in the end, you'll find yourself in a much **happier** place because of it...

Changing How Your Family Sees You

The inevitable thing *may* come that your family doesn't see the 'new you,' and you end up in an uphill struggle to convince *them* you're a changed person.

For example, the family may know you as a shy person.

Even though, you've done several years of self-confidence training, and are now a confident departmental manager of a store, just to give a real-world example.

But when you visit your family at the latest 'wedding do' they just see you as the shy person they've known all their life, EVEN if you're talking until you're breathless.

I've seen a similar situation to my own behaviour while I was changing as an individual.

The reason I included the '**Intro Going Outro**' chapter later in the book, is because I wanted to show you how I went from being shy to becoming a more resilient myself; the need to become more resilient in how I talked, interacted with people, and to be less affected by the words that are spoken or written by them.

That's also one of the interesting factors about the publishing community *too*.

You don't need so much as a "thick skin" to cope in it, but rather, you need "resilience."

The criticism you *can* receive, at times, for what you write, can be harsh.

I'm already aware what sort of criticism I *may* get for this book. It's likely this book will be received as being all over the place and stupid. But this book is more a "personal story" than a book meant as non-fiction teaching something in more abstract pen strokes. I want to inspire with my words…that's all.

However, the sort of commentary I may receive might include: *"This book wasn't written by someone who's an expert on relationships."*

If THIS is the criticism I'd get from how I wrote this book then the book isn't understood. This isn't a self-help book. It's a non-fictional memoir with elements of self-help used as an illustration.

It's a book about how one person dealt with life after divorce, and how she rebounded after it happened. It's supposed to be a book to inspire, to make you think about how you deal with your own life, to find elements with my story that will shape your own story of recovery…heartbreak DOESN'T last forever.

I worked 'damned hard' on making sure I healed my own heart because, as someone said to me once a decade ago: "Before you can love someone else properly once more you need to learn to love yourself again, and find yourself again and know what you'll want from the rest of your life."

The same goes with family in general.

You need to become resilient with them too. In fact, you need to learn to be resilient with them so you can be resilient in the wider world afterwards.

If I hadn't done this kind of action of learning a measure of resilience with family, I wouldn't have been able to find the way to be resilient as an author.

An author once said in an advert: "My mind is messy."

So yes, that's what you got when one author decided to verbalise her own life into a format that's a mixture of being a memoir and a bit of self-help. My real 'me' often gets responses such as "You helped me so much with your advice/words of encouragement/suggestions" that I felt compelled to do the same for people who might be going through a similar situation I was in a decade ago (*at the time of writing it was a decade ago.)

I stated before that family cannot be changed. Not everyone, and not always. It doesn't matter if that is going on.

The focus here is **YOU**.

If you want them to see you different you make the changes to be different in their minds. It's going to be a tough act to follow through but I can promise the end result will be self-satisfying.

Yes, you **can** put a *smug* smile on your face right now as you think how the "better you" *will* be perceived.

Hold your horses though. This change **does** come with one major clause in the contract.

I said, "better you."

That means **you** need to iron out any bad habits you have, and to do so you may need to even ask the family what they DON'T like about you.

For example, in **my** case, it was suggested that I had an annoying habit of blaming *others* for my mistakes. I assessed my behaviour, and have worked extensively on taking ownership of **my** actions.

I know already that *certain* family members will **be** blinkered, and **still** just see the 'person' who blamed others, but as the familiar (or not so familiar) saying goes: "Actions speak louder than words."

Talking of words, the other thing family would say is that I never finished anything I'd start...

You hold a FINISHED book in your hands. It's one of about a dozen finished books by the time my next birthday rolls around. In a way, I conquered the 'demons of my past' by doing the opposite of what my family expects.

Next on my list, is to get a job and do it for a few years besides the earlier suggestion of starting and running a business. It would give me the skills to succeed in the business I'm starting so I want to follow through with it.

Okay, enough of all the cliches and doing all the worst habits an author can have while writing a story, but I think I made my point here.

If you want the family to see the changed YOU, you need to take control and change them WITH YOU.

Most may realise you are a different person, and for the few who won't or refuse, you have the best option for you: walk away and leave them be.

Your best advocates to change their minds are your family who realises you are a different person and TELL the others of this change.

On the blank page, following this chapter, write a **few** of the habits and behaviours YOU know you have to change for your family to see you as a new person.

Be brutally **honest** with this process, or you *never* change yourself to a BETTER YOU!!!

This Page Left Intentionally Blank...
for you to write in.

Chapter Seven:

Grow For Your Future

Introduction

When I say 'Grow for your future' what I mean by this for you to *learn* from your mistakes, but also those made by the person who broke your heart.

Learn from what you feel that went wrong, and rise above it, and use it to **become** a better person.

I decided on this sentiment in the first few months of being alone while working on changing my mindset.

I realised fast that this sentiment must also be true in general about the person who had invested to spent their life with for a time with you for a time and that they need to change how they are if they want a new relationship…

To grow you need to **invest** in a few components that make you who you are.

One part of who you are is founded in your past experiences.

They start the moment you start to be self-aware and to be aware of those around you, such as your immediate family.

The next set of influences come from friends you start making when 'school' happens (preschool and onward).

Your interactions with society as a whole create another set of experiences, and they **can** be good and bad experiences.

But you have these experiences pretty much on a rolling basis.

For example, reading this book is creating an experience in your mind, and it may be a subconscious experience but it will be influencing you.

After all, you may have heard of the idea that you *can* end up being pulled into the world of a book and imagine being in the story being shown.

That's another example of the *same* principle I just suggested that **also** will influence you. That causes **different** people to like different books.

Taste is influenced by your past experiences, and you evolve your taste by any new experiences that haven't yet come into your life.

So, the idea of **growing my future** was formed from finding this mindset in myself. I'm going to go into the reasons *why* I became a forward-looking person rather than wanting to always look at the past.

The next subchapter **Put The Past In The Past** will describe why looking forward is a crucial component in 'moving on' from the heartbreak as well.

Growing can occur in many ways. One easy way is to become more intellectual in what you know and how much.

Skillshare and similar sites, YouTube, books, educational television programmes, studying for a degree, starting a new job, talking with people from *other* cultures, asking questions and listening (and learning) from the answers are just a few avenues to grow.

Another way to grow is to change how you see yourself in your self-image.

Yet another way is to put a value on your mental and emotional well-being and if either needs to be worked on, to invest in this.

Also, if you live with depression, anxiety or similar conditions the 'growing' part is also to accept you live with it and that there **are** reasons the condition may never go away. I live with depression and anxiety.

These conditions don't control me. **I control THEM.**

To grow past the point where they control you instead of you controlling them is the sort of mental growth you want to put a lot of work into, even if you don't have the conditions right now.

Understanding *what* causes a person to have these conditions *also* helps you to help someone with them.

Here are two things to remember about ANY mental or emotional conditions:

NEVER EVER apologise for having these conditions if you live with it, AND if you know someone with them NEVER

EVER force them to have to apologise for having it.

Note I call it a 'condition' and not an 'illness.'

That's a personal choice I made.

The reason for this is that I don't see them as something that makes me ill. I see it as something where my mind has stopped functioning in the way it was functioning before.

Similarly, I prefer to say of people in a wheelchair that they're "less able" because they still have partial or limited bodily function and often still can express emotions.

Being in the wheelchair doesn't make them unable to function as a human, it only makes them less able to do so.

And technology is fast catching up to give them more abilities…

So, rather than assuming your mind somehow is diseased (that word never sounds nice, don't you agree?) - by saying something like: *"I'm ill with depression"* **or** *"I'm ill with anxiety"* instead say of either: *"I have a condition causing me to feel depressed"* **or** *"I have a condition to feel anxiety."*

If asked what the condition is, just explain it as "more negative state of mind opposed to someone who is happy."

So, by explaining it this way you create a situation where you tell people "you are less able to feel happy."

But herein comes the idea of 'growing for your future'.

Whereas you cannot change how you feel you can CHANGE how you manage the feelings.

Here are MY power words: **I control my mind so I control the condition of my mind.**

Positive reinforcement is the medicine that can make your mind feel better about itself.

Remember that as you read on...

Put The Past In The Past

Immediately, I'll tell you there's a massive difference between reflecting on past events and applying it, often in a rather toxic way, in current situations. This rule of thumb applies to **all** situations really.

You don't start any new job with an immediate suggestion along the lines of: *"I had a bad boss so I'm sure my new boss here is a bad one too..."*

Right??

'Blame' is often the way that someone assigns the failure of something.

It doesn't matter what the "something" may be. It can be the loss of a job, the loss of a relationship, or anything else you can think of as a situation where another person is to blame for something you don't have anymore.

But who really is to blame if, for example, you lose a job?

You can say that the employer didn't like you, didn't want you, didn't appreciate you.

But if you're not suited for the job, you have to take responsibility for a part of the blame. Some people stay in their jobs for years or decades before retiring, but if this isn't the situation in your case then just move on to another job.

Each job brings its own challenges and knowledge to learn BUT if you just stick with it and keep moving forward you will eventually have the combination of knowledge, skills and experience to get a job where you are wanted for a long time.

Why *blame* for a lost job?

If you aren't wanted there treat it as an opportunity for ANOTHER employer to have **your** knowledge, skills and experience to benefit **them**.

A lost job is a learning experience, and not a sign that you suck at that particular job.

Right…?

If I were to go by **all** the lost jobs in my life (*plus* my original "failed" business that I had before the divorce happened, where my 'ex' had hampered in the efforts for to get it off the ground) you might think that I wouldn't end up as an author.

However, I did in the end and rather than assigning blame to the situation that existed back then I decided to pick it apart and look for all the parts that did work and did succeed despite it all, and construct a new business from it.

It took me almost five years to figure it all out, but in mid-2010 I got working on: "I'm going to start a business again."

I explained to my new guy what my ideas were, and he agreed they sounded good (he'd previously worked with his father in his father's business so had a business background). He and I agreed it would take time because we needed ideas for products, we needed to create a business plan, methodologies, all of it.

We immediately realised we needed to pick the plan apart and work out which parts we could do first, second, third, etc. The planning took a few years, but then in 2014, I had an epiphany…if you want to refer to it that way.

I'd been doing some creative writing (my real 'me' had) and I decided to work on stories. From this came another realisation that I could get back to my artwork and also doing photography as to additional "fundraising avenues."

Also, I didn't tell my new guy immediately that I had started writing. I didn't want him to put pressure on me. As I stated in the subchapter '**Changing How Your Family Sees You**' I had this habit to not complete things I'd do. I had to prove to myself that I had changed who I am, and so I set about writing.

My original goal was to just write 'a book' but then the book became 'a series' and because I'd witnessed the backstory of the game World of Warcraft grow I realised I wanted a bigger world for my books too, just like the game has. This was that caused the crucial change in me. I realised that the makers of the game couldn't have had their success if they'd just given up whenever going gets tough. I decided to learn from their success (and mistakes) and force myself to be different.

In 2015, I sat down to start writing the remaining 85% of the first book, and in early January 2016 I saw myself - the real 'me' - complete my first book.

That's when I put the past in the past. That's when I moved on from this blaming others for anything that might go wrong or bad in my life. I took responsibility for my actions.

And when the going got tough for me in respect of my book writing I wasn't afraid to ask for help OR to admit that I had made the mistakes. I didn't blame anyone other than myself…

Similarly, with my life, in general, I've gone from 'always blaming others' to 'take responsibility, learn from it, move on a better person approach.'

"He who doesn't learn from the past is going to repeat it." ~ Santaya

This phrase has many variations of it, and this is the one I most commonly use. I use it as power words to remind me that I MUST learn from MY past so not to repeat anything I did the wrong way. One part of learning from the past is to learn to keep the past in the past.

Learn from it but don't assume that you can change it and what happened in the past happened to you, and you should take ownership of it and make it a tool to be a better person…

The Here and Now

Life will feel like it's in a turmoil right now. In fact, life is just all one turmoil after another. Life gets hectic and it can get too much at times.

When it does you just need to allow yourself to slow down.

The mind can be so beautiful really. It's capable of complex thought. It can reason with logic. It can be creative in so many ways.

We have billions of examples of human's endeavour to use their mind for creating art, literature, scientific discoveries, philosophic theory and much more.

In the grander scheme of everything, each individual's place is tiny in comparison.

But each individual is still important for the grander scheme.

All what I just said *may* sound like some odd sort of philosophy really but in a way that's how I view the world we live in.

To me, every person is important and has something to contribute.

To me, it's sad when a person doesn't reach his or her full potential for any number of reasons; with the worst reason being the idea that they somehow decide that others around them don't matter for reasons they only understand.

This is the 'crazy' world I was staring out on whenever I did look out of my window in the first year or so after I was alone.

Well, *not* completely alone because I'd met my new guy halfway through **that** year, and this was making my world spin around so fast that it was impossible to figure out feelings from one day to the next…

When I realised I was 'in love' again that is when a different realisation started to present itself.

There's a purpose *why* this subchapter is in the middle of the seventh chapter. It's the seventh month, in about the middle of the month, that the first feeling of 'in love' emerged.

I was *only* capable of really telling him a month or more **later** it had been happening…

The question that was popping into my mind over and over again at the time was: "How am I feeling in the here and now?"

The next question to follow the *first* question was: "What about tomorrow, next week, a month or a year from now?"

My new guy fell in love with me **first**.

My new guy **still** tells me he fell in love with me in a matter of days or a few weeks. It took me longer because I was still reeling from a broken heart. I had not discovered yes that my heart could be unbroken, healed, fixed, etc.

But, oh boy, when I woke up and I felt like life **could be** okay again, that's when I realised that in all the turmoil of life I found something peaceful again…

Love is an extremely peaceful feeling. It heals, nourishes and sustains us when we receive it.

But not so when it's gone.

If you have seen (or even if you've not seen it you may have heard of the movie) but I will include a little something appropriate from the story from the third Star Wars movie, The Revenge of the Sith.

In almost the last scene of the movie Padmé Amidala falls 'out of love' because of what she's told by Anakin Skywalker. Her heart breaks in that scene and it leads to her death later on. It's a scene that feels emotionally close to me because I felt similar on the day and at the moment I was told the words that had broken my heart.

But right now, at the time of writing, I look back at how it was for me back then, and now I feel now, and I have to admit that breaking my heart actually started the process of changing me into the person that WOULD make my new guy fall in love with me.

That's why it's so important to re-evaluate the 'here and now' constantly. It changes. It evolves. I can be better.

The turmoil, for me, isn't entirely gone yet. I'm still healing from the hurt. But every day I'm a tiny bit closer to a day when I wake up and I'm at peace with myself, and that's when I can start to take action for better things. I'll describe my plans in the next chapter.

In the meantime, YOU write your plan of action for better things for yourself at the end of this chapter. We'll compare notes at the end of the chapter and see how similar or different the plan of action is for each of us.

Note that I say 'plan *of* action' and NOT 'plan *for* action.' There's a **reason** for this that will become clear as you read on…

Take Action For Better Things

When you sorted out everything about your life. And that day will come sooner rather than later, it is time to start to put your action plan to work…

Wait, you say you haven't got one? You were waiting for me to tell you this stuff now…?

You hold your action plan in your hands.

It's **this** book.

Obviously, you decided you needed someone to do some major pep talk or else you wouldn't have bought this book.

Through these pages, I'm your new best friend who tells you to get up, get doing everything you ever wanted to do.

Because they didn't happen while you were married it gives YOU the perfect EXCUSE to do it now…or at least get started with it now.

Yes, welcome to the mindset of a person who decided to be so different that she ended up 'scaring' the 'ex' when he did decide to pay a visit.

I'm not going into what happened (that's private) **but** from my perspective, it was awfully **funny**.

I found it *more* fun than I should have done so at the time; yes, it *was* a rather laughable situation at best.

It felt **good** to be in control instead of him wanting to dictate what would **or** wouldn't happen.

But the end result was **me** making a decision. I had **enough** on the possibility of him 'turning up' out of the blue, and pestering me.

The real "me" is **now** living with my new guy because of the decision, and she has lived this new life now for several years.

Life is a lot more peaceful now. The worries are mostly gone. I'm with a person who loves me, and whom I CAN love fully and unconditionally. I know he does the same…

That's what I mean by taking action for better things.

Sometimes you **have** to leave behind the things that feel familiar and embrace, instead, the unfamiliar.

It helps with how you feel and how you act.

As a species, the human is unlike any other species that we know of in that it can create a reason to exist. Compare this with dogs who live in the moment.

As humans, we can create (or break) the reason for existing with our actions. At least I believe this is part of how we act as a species.

It *can* be a scary thought to move on and to start over. But if you build yourself a network of support before and after you do this you CAN cope with it.

Family, friends, colleagues at work (old or new), various organisations that offer this sort of help are all there for helping you.

If you're moving on *because* you met that **new** person that's the best reason for this action.

Looking at the situation in perspective I do realise I should have done things differently in some cases, however, the outcome would possibly have taken a lot longer time to achieve. And a small part of me even wonders if some of what I have now may never have come to pass…

Yes, that's a tough question to answer. It isn't good to say "If I did this then this or that might be different…"

If you get yourself into this mode of thinking you'll start second guessing everything and every choice you make.

The better option is to plan outcomes for a period of time. So, for example, say that by a certain date you have achieved such and such goal. For me, one such goal was to be debt-free. I actually managed to get there with the help from my new guy, and now he and I are working on doing the same for him…

This is where a partnership with a new person in your life is a better option, especially if, like it was in my case, you had someone around who didn't really think in these terms.

If you're not in any relationship *yet*, you want to make it **clear** that you believe in a relationship that equals partnership.

I actually *know* of people who claim that a woman should be putting the needs of the man she's with first, however, I'm going to say to you that, from personal experience, this is the <u>worst</u> thing for the longterm success of your relationship.

My relationship with my new guy IS **strong** BECAUSE we are partners, because we treat one another as equals, because we look out for one another's needs, and because we give and take equally…

Heartbreak is generally caused by **not** being treated in this sort of way - this being treated with kindness, equality or as a partner - by a person who's supposed to love you **unconditionally**.

When your love interest is not treating you with unconditional love in mind, the love isn't going to be as perfect as a situation where it is happening.

Unconditional has to mean <u>precisely</u> that. But if you *want* to receive such love you should also *give* it in a similar way back to him (or her).

So one other way to take action for better things is to establish from the start WHAT you want to get from the relationship.

Don't hesitate to tell what these conditions are. Yes, it sounds harsh when I say it in this way but I'm hammering home a point here.

If the person you've met is hesitant about accepting these conditions, you can just adapt without changing the conditions but never forget what it is you want from the relationship.

The three things I told my new guy I wanted was trust, honesty and to be shown love by him.

I mentioned earlier about "show versus tell" in the context of a story in a book. I suggest now that this kind of thing also applies to real life too.

This is the **precise** reason why you need to take action on building your future in the way you want it to be.

The future may never be perfect. There will be ups and downs.

But you **can** set the "rule book" up from this moment *before* you get into your next relationship.

Take on board something my new guy said to me: "I saw a personality I could fall in love with, so I fell in love completely. I knew I wanted to be with this person I'd met because of how she behaves and how she treats those around her."

The reason why my new guy was invested in a successful relationship from day one is that I had taken action for better things for myself.

Changing how I behaved as well as being certain that I didn't want the same as what my 'ex' had done put me in that "good place" for him to fall in love with me.

Remember also what someone said to me about loving myself first before loving someone else again?

That's also part of this better future…

I bet you're now a lot more invested in creating the best future for yourself after this personal story from the "real me" *(this is probably only part of the book where I'm going to dedicate a whole subchapter about the real me).*

Now draw a massive heart below on the blank part of this page and write your first name inside it. That's who it is you are going to love FIRST…

Future PROOF

Ten years ago (almost) my life started to **change**. As I write this book. I'm **amazed** that it's just a few months from now that it's a decade ago that I first met my **new guy**.

I'm not going to into the method of *how* we met (that's the story my real "me" is going to write into a book - it will be love story), but I **will** say that life went *so* much different from what I was assuming it to *be* like on that last day of August 2017…

I sat in a silent house when my 'ex' had left finally at around 11 PM on that day. I'm not kidding you that silence can be deafening.

Silence can be deafening for a mind that's reeling from the *loss* caused by a relationship ending.

What I **didn't** know in those few lonely hours, was that approximately seven months later, I'd meet someone **by chance.**

It would lead to the life I have now; a life of love, happiness and friendship.

It was the first day of my future and I **didn't** know it yet.

I had no forewarning that I could meet someone. I will say that the circumstances could have gone two directions: either we'd be just friends OR the love life we now enjoy.

I didn't even want to think about the possibility of not being friends with this person I had met by chance. And *then*, there was the possibility of feeling more for this guy.

But that was back then…

Now, I'm actually looking forward to the future I have ahead of me. I enjoy my life and it's blessed with love and happiness.

There's a phrase I like: **proof of concept**.

The meaning of these words literally means: "A realisation of a certain method or idea to demonstrate it's feasibility" (as listed on Wikipedia).

Nothing of my life before was a proof of concept as to how my life would be like for me later. It did, however, give me the knowledge and foresight of how I didn't want the situation to be.

I wanted a better future, and identifying this became a bit of an obsession.

I *alluded* at the process of changing my mind, and this is the end result of a process I *had* started on **that** lonely night alone. I spoke of nurturing your mind when you find yourself alone. This is where the process of finding a proof of concept of **HOW** a relationship should be like came from.

For me it did. So should it do for you…

The idea of "future proof" means simply this: you build a future that is secure emotionally.

The idea behind this idea comes from a source you're already aware of and that is "having a pension." That's your financial future proof. But to **do** the same with your emotions you need to take a similar approach and invest in a future where you know where you stand in terms of your emotions.

This Page Left Intentionally Blank…
for you to write in.

Chapter Eight:

Finding Help By

Helping Yourself

Introduction

The **best** way to help yourself, when the going gets tough, is to acknowledge that you **can** help yourself. Ignoring your feelings by suggesting that everything is okay isn't good.

Some of the best help came when I acknowledged that I needed the help. I sought the help from a counsellor with whom I could speak about my feelings, about my past, about my hopes, and never be judged for anything I said.

I could cry as much as I wanted without being told it is stupid or similar.

The reason why it was better, and easier, to speak to a stranger is that they weren't closely tied to my life.

She helped me immensely with sorting out my mind, for me to realise I could BE helped, that my life could BE better than it was.

Some of what I said in the **Family vs Family** chapter directly ties in with what I was doing during these six months of my life. The counsellor intended for **me** to be given the tools to help myself. This *may* differ from counsellor to counsellor though.

When you look for a counsellor I'd go for an informal talk to determine you can get along with him or her. Often, the greatest proportion of the "help" comes not from them *but* from your **own** perceptions of the visits.

Self-help is the biggest and most important component whenever you **need** help. The earliest component of this self-help is to acknowledge that you need the help.

When you come to this realisation, and in my case, it happened while my 'ex' was still active in my life, you want to look for the right sort of help.

In a marriage breakup, it's essential to have a lawyer to guide you through the legal minefield, but you should never ignore your emotional or mental needs.

*As I'm no lawyer I cannot give guidance, and as this book is intended as a universal book to be read by people in different parts of this world, the scope of the book is more about the emotional and mental guidance I **can** create by sharing my own story.*

What I **will** say about getting a lawyer is to seek out BEFORE the split-up happens so the lawyer **can** educate you about what the law says about a marriage break-up, so they can tell you what your rights are, what you can do to protect your own needs.

Protecting your children against the upset of a divorce should start early too, and is a very important part of the process.

When my lawyer started telling me about the divorce law I decided to keep reading, and to a degree, I think that this reading is what gave me the knowledge to fight against the suggestions or misinformation my 'ex' wanted to convince me to be fact.

It's important to be aware of what is a **fact**, compared to what may be a *lie*.

It's important to the society we **all** live in that we're aware of facts, but it becomes more personal when you know something to be a fact and someone you loved tries to convince it is all lies.

Becoming more knowledgeable will help you. It applies to everything in your life.

Knowing divorce law better makes certain you understand what goes on better in the proceedings.

Understanding financial structures, such as loans, savings accounts, investing and others, will make it easier to do what I suggested in the subchapter **Future PROOF**.

To learn more about nutrition and exercise makes you capable of being healthier and fitter.

It's true of ANYTHING you do. You don't need to work on getting a degree to make yourself more knowledgeable, though you can go down this route, and if you want to do this, then go for it…

It's OKAY To Ask For Help

When you're in trouble you should always ask for help. For example, if you're at school and you don't know a math sum you'd raise your hand and ask the teacher for help.

If you're trying to learn a new skill you'd seek out websites or YouTube videos to explain things further.

An example of where this works so well is the world of book writing. There are thousands and thousands of websites and YouTube videos these days teaching every aspect of this industry.

Personally, I've *probably* only learned a fraction of all the skill one needs for this sort of job, but I know I can find more information and keep learning by just opening my browser.

Similarly, when your emotions are all over the place for one reason or another, you shouldn't stop yourself from asking help… **EVER.** The **best** help comes from some professional, and I encourage to find such help if you need it.

Occasionally, you'll notice how a person says "I can cope with…" (whatever it may be they're suggesting as something they can cope with). I spoke earlier about resilience.

This is a trait that doesn't to every person with ease, and how resilient you are is conditioned by your upbringing as well as factors you encounter in your life outside your home.

In my opinion, and this is based entirely on observation of people (which I enjoy doing and which is possibly one reason why my real "me" does such good characterisation) is that there are three broad groups of people in terms of resilience.

I belong in the middle group right now, but my own 'membership' is **easily** interchangeable based on current situations or circumstances.

These groupings aren't "set in stone", but a temporary condition we can find ourselves in depending on the events of a given day:

1) Those who can cope with their current situation as well as the bad situations that present themselves.

Remember the wheel I mentioned in subchapter **Is my life worth living?**…this is the TOP of the wheel. This is when life is at its best. You're happy. Life is going excellent. You're thriving…

2) The "middle crowd" (as I tend to call it) which consists those individuals who are coping but their life has many fast ups and downs to it.

But overall, they're **not** in a bad place, but also **not** really in a good place. Life is a challenge but they often have the mechanisms to cope their way through it.

They *can* find themselves in the life of point 1 OR point 3 if circumstances change.

This, in fact, is the **normal** position to be in for most of your life (even *if* you live with depression or anxiety really, as I do).

3) When life is at its worst you belong in the third group. Remember that you don't stay in this group all the time. It's where you go "to take a break" from life or when something happens that pulls the rug from under your feet.

This may be where you **are** right now with your heartbreak…

Or you feel like you **are** in this place right now, and if you are there are several things to remember. Remember that the feelings don't last, and you shouldn't dwell on them.

Asking for help is tough for all of us. The place where it is toughest is when it involves a relationship shattering to pieces. A relationship is regarded as private, and it's not something to put through the wringer (to use a negative expression to push a point).

Personally, my new guy and I don't like to put our relationship out in the public, which was why I wrote this book under an assumed pen name.

I'm also writing a book above the 'story of love' between my new guy and I. Both this book and that one have my new guy's blessing.

When I told him the idea of this book his reaction was actually different from what I expected. He suggested that he had learned from ME about having a good relationship with other people.

He admits that before he met me he would have "awkward moments" with his own parents (this is the best I *can* explain it without saying what they were).

Basically speaking, he'd "avoid" them for periods of time. I think his mother was the first to notice he's different now. He said her attitude towards him was different because he had learned to be LESS confrontational towards him.

I told you before that I don't like any form of conflict.

Asking for help *is* another way to **avoid** conflict. It allows people to see that you **do** have vulnerabilities, and having them is perfectly fine (as I will discuss in the next subchapter **Emotions Will Heal You**). By asking for help when it's needed you stabilise your life and give yourself the tools to grow.

Emotions Will Heal You

If **anyone** ever claims that crying makes you a weak person or, as a guy - if you ARE guy reading this book by chance - you should remember that the idea presented by the society that shedding tears is bad, stupid, or only what girls do this, **is NOT valid**.

My response to **you** is that having emotions - *not* the negative emotion such as anger - but *instead* being able to feel empathy, cry, or **show** genuine happiness **is** something that actually makes you the **strongest** individual.

Doesn't a parent cry when they see their newborn for the first?

Don't people cry when mourning a loved one?

But *often* they forget the time in between.

They forget that **having** emotions binds us together as social beings. Life isn't just about always smiling and saying "cheese" for photos.

If you're a guy, especially, and someone says something hurtful to you then you have the RIGHT to be upset.

For both men **and** women, it's HOW you express the feeling that shows your **strength.**

Never speak words in anger in this situation.

Instead, you can request the person doesn't behave like this and then just walk away. They're not worth any additional moment of your time.

I remember a time when I felt much upset in my daily life. My 'ex' would then start to argue with me, often also for no reason. I'm not one to want that (which is why my current relationship is so perfect as my new guy doesn't like it either) so instead of joining into the argument I'd walk away.

That apparently would make my 'ex' angrier, because he'd start to bang a wall and shout at me about doing this 'so he wouldn't hit me'.

By the way, just so you know, he **never** did hit me. But the words, where he would say this to me, **did** hurt me deeply.

The internal scars in my memory, my mental well-being and my emotions, are present to this day.

It's this *why* I felt compelled to write this book in ANOTHER name so to protect myself against him.

Yes, I know that perhaps a day will come when I have to "come out" and tell the world who "N. Lee" really is (especially if this book became so popular that it hits the bestseller lists) but until such time I'll stay anonymous.

That brings me to another matter…

I know there are guys out there who don't want to be that 'tough guy' and who just want to get along with others and for that I commend you. But then someone may come along and hurt you.

Often in today's society, it's forgotten that guys can have emotions **too**.

They **can** feel upset so they cry, and I think it's often done in secret as people associate shame with a guy crying.

There is NOTHING shameful for **you**, as a guy, to be crying.

In fact, I will assure you that good emotions - such as crying - **can** do you a world of good if you let yourself do this emotion…

However, anger **can** be a healthy emotion *if* you don't express it with negativity. Anger *can* be expressed by being **against** a bad situation.

An example of how it *can* be positive can be the "anger" you feel that causes you to join in a protest march because you saw or heard something that isn't good.

The **cost** of negative anger is great to your emotional well-being.

It's an emotion that causes many problems and may have been the reason *why* you found yourself with your heart broken.

It's certain to have contributed to the failure, and then the end, of your relationship.

It's a reactive emotion, so if one person starts to express this sort of anger it's likely that the other person does the same.

I found myself reacting to my 'ex' whenever **he** became angry.

My reaction wasn't anger.

As someone who has always *hated* conflict, I reacted to his behaviour with deep sadness. A dream of "growing old" had been broken, and thus it broke my heart.

And to be blunt to myself, and also to show you how *blame* plays a role here, I **did** blame him for the end of the relationship.

But later on, when I was able to analyse the situation and realised that my *own* mistakes were what may have caused the situation in the first place.

Apart from the few bits and pieces of the past described in the book I'll refrain from telling how and why because that's stuff that's too personal really.

Nowadays I don't feel the sense of blaming myself, because I know now that it *was* inevitable for the relationship to end, and I've grown past these feelings of anger, sadness and pain as I went through the processes described in the first two chapters of this book.

Equal to anger, there are other reactive emotions. Sadness, happiness and indifference are also reactive emotions.

Now I bet the question you're asking is how "indifference" - yes, that meme where someone may go **"meh!"** at a situation - is an emotion.

Lacking emotion can almost be an emotion too because you're not reacting to a situation either in a good or a bad way. Though a specialist with a psychology background would dismiss this suggestion immediately. This is a personal viewpoint rather than me opposing known science.

Being indifferent **is** a negative emotion **too** in my opinion. Okay, I'm no psychologist and this is just my own interpretation of the way emotions work.

So, to give context, I think indifference to negative things **is** something that's happening to our society, together with *too* much negative emotion. You're smart enough to figure out what sort of things happening in our society I'm referring to…

But with all that reasoning explained, here's why it's so **important** for men (and boys too) to express emotions, such as sadness and happiness, without it being made out to be wrong, bad or stupid by anyone around them.

These emotions are a **good** counter-balance for anger.

In my opinion, they help to soften the impact of anger, and thus make anger into a more positive emotion, rather than it being used in a negative way.

When my new guy realised how very hurt I'd been by my 'ex' it brought tears to his eyes. On that day and in that moment, he promised he'd help to heal *my* heart.

He still doesn't totally realise that my heart began to heal when I saw him being able to show a reaction to pain, even if the pain wasn't his own.

In the subchapter **How can I change how I behave?** I started the chapter with the **very** word that's OUTCOME of knowing how to show positive emotion: COMPASSION.

A person who has learned to access positive emotions also knows that the balancing emotion of compassion can reset emotions from going negative.

This is **why** I also suggested that walking away from an argument is good. It's another way for two people to reset their emotions.

A boy, who learns that crying is a positive emotion and an emotion that's good for them, has, therefore, an **easier** time to be less prone to conflict and negative emotion.

No one who cries does this to be stupid.

It's done to give the mind an outlet for the pain caused by a situation, or as stated, to feel compassion or similar feeling for those around them…

New Meaning of 'It Takes Two To Tango'

When an argument happens, usually, people say this saying: *"It takes two to tango."*

Usually, this statement has a negative connotation connected to it, because it will imply that it's about two people feeding one another with negative energy by arguing.

However, I can suggest to you that this statement **can** have a more positive version instead.

Rather than using this to cause conflict, it's better used to cause more harmony in the world at large and to bring harmony into your personal life.

You are at the driving seat of making this happen.

However, in a relationship, you do want to **yield** and **allow** the other person in the relationship to take the driving seat instead. It feels nice to be supported by someone.

This goes for **both** individuals in the relationship.

I stated that I value **trust, honesty** and **loyalty**. These **are** the "DNA" of a good relationship. Any of them. Family. Friends. Your "true love"…

Cue the best "true love" words from 'The Princess Bride.'

"Love is many things none of them logical."
— William Goldman, The Princess Bride

Yes, a relationship isn't logical in the slightest.

Break-up is even more illogical.

But when you're ready for a new relationship the BEST way to get over the broken heart is to let it be healed by someone you've met. Let them take the driving seat, and let them pull you up to the light, and start to make you find your mojo again…

Communication Is King

One of the **best** things that my current guy and I **share** is that we talk a lot about stuff…all the time.

He listens to me when I tell him things. I listen to him when he tells me things.

We discuss difficult topics, such as finance, as mentioned before.

We talk to find a resolution if we notice some sort of problem, either between us or with someone else or with some sort of situation.

We talk until we solve the issue, and then we talk to lighten the mood and get back to what we're best at having fun with one another.

It was US always talking which got my partner ALSO into story writing in the end…

When he started to see I was working on book writing he would occasionally say: *"If I did a story I would have it be about such and such..."* and initially I'd just listen with interest until **one day** I responded with: *"When..."*

A simple word that starts to open up the world of being an author to him *too*.

A simple word *can* alter so much.

Or a **few**.

When someone says "I love you" it changes things. The opposite can be true too.

Being told that **you** weren't loved any more, was probably the most painful day of **your** life. It was the same for **me**...

But words *can* have healing power.

For me, the healing power started to come *when* my new guy told me, regardless of how I might *feel* about him, that he'd always *be* there for me; and help me in *any* way possible.

...and that he'd **love** me even if I'd never love him back...

Yes, those were his actual words and they brought tears to my eyes, and they caused me to start to have similar feelings for him...

Words **can** create trust between people. *And* a whole lot of **good** feelings, happiness and other positive events in your life.

But the wrong words, or those spoken with anger, can also break trust **too**.

Broken trust causes doubt to set in, and then you can't keep a relationship going. Every time I hear the story of someone who had the trust they felt for someone else BROKE they had to leave the relationship behind.

The flip side of this is that giving trust to others can pull people TO you. You can gain friends, respect and a lot more other good stuff from giving trust.

Okay, you've been told that trust is earned and *not* given. That's **true**.

But **don't** assume you always have to make a person earn this trust from you. **Sometimes** it's good to let them get *your* trust unconditionally…

Communication is used for many varying reasons.

It's used for exchanging ideas, and this is *how* society became so diverse as it's now. It will be obvious that, like within our society, good communication leads to better relations. When people talk it's more likely they find a middle ground and therefore have less conflict. It's when humans **talk** that it excels at being the **best**. It leads to innovations, new ideas, inventions, new creativity, and so much more.

The **same** is true of a relationship, and when the people in a relationship TALK, they create the path towards something **greater** than themselves.

The **best** moments of my own life is when I sit with my new guy and we just talk endlessly…

This Page Left Intentionally Blank…
for you to write in.

Chapter Nine:

Foodies 'n

Nutrition

Introduction

Food **can** play a major role in *how* you feel in your everyday life. When you're depressed you **will** eat to give yourself a sense of comfort.

I can identify with you if this is something you feel compelled to do. Because I've eaten in a similar way to give myself comfort in the first days and weeks after I was alone, though the feeling of needing to eat for comfort lessened as soon as I started having the sense of friendship with my new guy.

So this illustrates to a degree that there is a correlation between how we eat and whether we're happy or sad about the people have in our lives.

I **believe** we eat in *this* way because our body, somehow, knows that it's lacking the nutrients and vitamins it needs for us to *be* well.

The condition causing us to be depressed or anxious is both a physical and a mental condition; it's not just something going on in your mind nor should you be told to ignore it when the warning signs are there that you have either of these (or any related) conditions.

In the subchapter **Mind Over Mind**, I stated this: *"When you want to change you can influence your mind into a different mindset."*

To alter how you eat your food you **need** to alter the mindset related to this.

So changing your mind for you to see food in a different way will help you, in the long run, to keep healthy.

But let's start with a fundamental moment of you accepting the following power words: **To make your mind well you need to work on making your body well, and to make your body well you need to make your mind well.**

In the subchapter **Mind Over Mind**, I suggested that a *changed* mindset is needed to make you think 'differently' about people around you.

However, you should also apply the **same** ideas to food, too.

It's fine to eat for comfort as long as you don't ever overdo it. You should check your height, current weight, and then adjust your eating habits to those factors.

There's a certain amount of calories we should ingest daily, and my doctor told me the following:

"When you're eating you should always make sure that half your plate is filled with vegetables, and that reduce all your portions by two spoonfuls."

I'm not an expert on food, but I **do** understand that eating healthier means I **can** maintain a healthier mind and body.

You need to adjust the amount you consume if you want to lose weight.

Generally **increasing** your intake of vegetables and **decreasing** your protein intake does the trick in first controlling your weight, and then by reducing the intake somewhat, you can allow it to start to drop. You'll also want to watch your intake of bread, pasta and potato.

My own food intake is based around what's eaten in the Mediterranean (also known as the 'Mediterranean diet') that consists of using olive oil, eating vegetables from the region, eating plenty of oily fish types, and being generous with the intake of fresh tomatoes.

Sweet products like desserts, sweets and chocolate, biscuits and cake, ice cream and other such items are also on your "be careful with this list."

You CAN give yourself comfort food but make it a healthier option. Occasionally eating a savoury cracker, or eating raisins and nuts, or an apple is better comfort food…

Chocolate Is Nutrition...

Sometimes!

I often will call myself a 'reformed chocoholic'. I love chocolate *but* these days I've decided on a more holistic and rational approach to this food.

I don't eat it **because** I want to be healthier.

To be healthier means losing weight (for me). I do that by not eating the wrong food.

Sometimes indulging in "naughty foods" is **fine** and even something that is encouraged by some nutritionists who will say that occasionally indulging makes it easier to lose weight.

So actually, there's **no** "naughty food" though you can be naughty with food.

This is how I see 'eating food'. Or else, why would it be called "junk food?"

Occasionally having a bit of chocolate to eat, or some cola to drink, or a piece of cake to sink your teeth in, or ice cream to savour - rather doing this all the time - promotes a sense of reward in your mind.

Yes, there's *that* mind again; a mind that **can** do so many wondrous things for us all…

In doing so, because you do eat the naughty stuff, but not all the time, your mind tricks your body into believing it's receiving loads and loads of **yummy** food.

In reality, you're not eating much and on this power trip of weight loss.

Just remember that starving equates anorexia and that's NOT good for you (neither is forcing yourself to throw up the food).

If you do EITHER please go see your doctor for specialist help with it.

I'd rather have my readers healthy and eating *with* purpose instead (see the next subchapter **'Get Cooking, Eat Yourself Healthier'** for ideas for how I did this myself).

But do feel free to indulge, and what experts tend to say when they include "indulging" in their dieting advice. They will say that indulging makes dieting easier.

Chocolate is a contentious food. Some people say it's bad for you, while others will say it's good for you. Some people even break it down to which type you eat as to whether it's good or bad for you.

The research boils down to the research done into **what** chocolate is made of.

Chocolate is produced from roasted and ground cacao seeds.

It's a foodstuff that was known to the original indigenous people of modern-day Mexico of as early as 1,900 BC.

Even the two associated words come from ancient word known in the local language: kakawa (cacao) and chocolātl (chocolate). Yes, I have a keen interest in the origins of words. Something that's also very evident in a lot of my storytelling done by the real "me."

Chocolate is an energy-rich food, and eating it in large quantities without exercising **often** isn't good for **anyone**. But the food has been shown to have 'cocoa flavanols', and they're shown to improve blood pressure levels and be good for your heart if consumed moderately.

Like with all foods, moderation is **best**…

So if I'm so concerned with being healthy why would I eat chocolate?

I'm certain you're asking this question now, especially as I just contradicted my earlier suggestion of **not** eating chocolate any more. But, remember what I said about indulging. I read the information about the benefits of chocolate and gave myself permission to INDULGE.

You should do that **too**.

Improve your eating habits and then give yourself similar permission.

By doing such an action you're adding yet another component to changing your mindset. This time it's a component that influences how you feed yourself...

But why am I discussing chocolate so extensively when I easily could have talked about not eating junk food? I said earlier that this book is about creating a positive story for you to draw inspiration from. So, talking about a food that is beneficial for you, even if it's classed as a "junk food" if eaten in larger quantity gives you an example of how to evaluate the food you eat.

By re-evaluating one food, you now can do the SAME with every other food you eat and create a picture from it similar to how the police might build a picture from a crime scene. You can apply the process described here to every food.

In the next subchapter, I'll give you an insight into my eating habits in terms of meals...

Get Cooking, Eat Yourself Healthier

I stated earlier that I draw inspiration for my eating habits from the foods commonly eaten in the Mediterranean, also commonly referred to as the "Mediterranean diet."

This is a diet that's primarily based on eating fruits and vegetables, certain whole grains, legumes and nuts.

You'd cook with olive oil, and will flavour foods primarily with herbs and spices rather than salt. It also consists of eating more starchy foods such as bread and pasta.

You'd include fish, especially an oily fish such as salmon, replacing most meat with the fish.

I quoted earlier the direct suggestion of filling half my plate with vegetables.

Fresh vegetables are the best nutrient in your diet because they offer many of the vitamins, minerals and natural acids our bodies rely on to be healthy.

There is a lot of evidence that shows a direct link between the **health** of your brain and **what** you eat.

It has been shown through extensive studies that the people living around the Mediterranean Sea, such as the Spanish, southern French, Italian and Greek - probably **all** the other nations bordering the sea - have a diet that contributes to *many* of them growing gracefully to old age.

The first ingredient in my kitchen is olive oil; it is produced by pressing whole olives.

It can be used for cooking by frying vegetables or meat or fish, or it can be used as a salad dressing.

The regions in which the olive trees grow generally have seen the harvest of this food for well over the last 10,000 years (as identified by archaeological digs), so it's obvious that the ancient human must have known there was a special, healthy property to the food.

Tomatoes are the edible red berry (fruit) of the tomato plant. Based on its origins, it isn't strictly a Mediterranean food, but I include it because of the health benefits it offers.

However that said, it *did* make its way to the Mediterranean region in the mid-1500s.

They can be eaten raw or cooked, and there are many modern varieties.

Typically, you'll find plum tomatoes used in my kitchen for sauces, or cherry tomatoes halved and added at the end of the cooking process for a nice sharp contrasting taste.

In terms of oily fish, I prefer salmon which I will steam wrapped in foil together with sliced onion and herbs.

Typically, my new guy and I will eat anything from 400 to 700 grams (about 1 to 1½ pound) of vegetables a day. *We* prefer to be "full" from eating a lot of vegetables, and only a little bit of meat or fish and only a little bit of pasta (or on certain occasions some rice or potatoes).

In all cases, it's better to eat fresh food over processed food (prepared meals, tinned food, or fast food).

Often, well actually ALWAYS, these processed foods have too much salt in them, and they may have artificial components in them masquerading as "healthy" when they are actually very unhealthy for us - remember what I suggested about food in the previous subchapter:

Like with all foods, moderation is best…

Having a pizza or your favourite burger SHOULD also be treated as indulging yourself, just what I said about chocolate.

There is a reason WHY I include a chapter about nutrition in a book about finding yourself again after heartbreak. It's because you need to TAKE CARE of yourself in more ways than just recovering from the heartbreak, and being healthy is one way.

I started the book with the suggestion of sorting out your mindset by changing how you think as well as how you treat your mind. But being healthy in your eating habits DOES make both of these actions so much easier…

Cooking your meals, especially doing it together as a couple, has **other** benefits as well for both individuals doing it.

A kitchen is a good place for talking, for cracking jokes, for being silly, for exchanging ideas.

Some of the ideas the real "me" has come up with for books come from talking in this way with my new guy.

Cooking can also be relaxing in some ways, and any activity that relaxes you is beneficial to your body but also to your mind. Your mind benefits from relaxation by being healthier.

The stress-part of depression and anxiety is reduced by being healthier.

So just like a game of knocking over dominoes you are building a healthier YOU that will have longterm benefits.

For me, this is an ongoing process. Every day I knock over another of these 'domino' pieces, and every day I know I get a bit healthier.

But the evidence of "eating yourself healthier" comes from a better place. It has been suggested to my new guy that his Type 2 diabetes is GOING DOWN ever so slowly, and has been doing for the last few years. The timeline of this happening correlates with how long we've eaten the Mediterranean diet.

When you discover a good thing, you repeat it…right?

So drop anything bad habits… I'll tell you the next mindset I developed to do this for myself, and *why* I keep drinking cola as MY indulgence food…

Breaking Old Habits

The process of first reducing and then eliminating so-called "bad food" literally started a few days after my "ex" had left. In addition to clearing out all his belongings, he had decided also to take with him all the food we still had in the house.

When my mother heard of this "dilemma" she paid for me to have food in the house…

My mother is a stickler for what to eat.

With her in tow, shopping for food meant I had to be picky.

I own many cookbooks so before she arrived I went through these for ideas for meals that were cheap to make - she couldn't spend a big pile of money for food so I had to have a precise list.

It was in one of my cookbooks that I came across the term "Mediterranean diet."

It was finding this information that started the process of changing my mindset about the **sort** of food I eat. So, while in the shop, I purchased a bag of wholemeal pasta, a few tins of oily fish (cheaper than fresh fish), a range of vegetables, some wholemeal bread, milk and suggested to her - *cautiously* - the suggestion of indulging in "a food," and she agreed that I could buy a single one-litre bottle of cola...

Fast forward to a few years later, and I'm moving in with my new guy.

Between that day in the shop with my mother and the day of moving in with my new guy, I'd become more and more aware of the **benefits** of eating a Mediterranean diet.

When I suggested to my new guy that we should base our diet around this style of eating he was immediately interested.

What neither of us realised at the time is that eating healthier and wanting to do this changes the mind in terms of how it thinks about fast food or junk food.

In the meantime, I had seen the information suggesting about having food that's your indulgence food. It used to be chocolate, but now it's cola. Though that said I have made a vow to eliminate ALL junk food, ALL fast food and ALL so-called indulgence from my diet in 2019.

Because I've been moving into a mindset that can cope without these foods over a long time I know I can do the elimination with relative ease...

So don't rush yourself in changing how you eat. Learn to eat better at the same time as you learn a new mindset for yourself. It WILL get noticed if you are doing things to "take care of yourself..."

The World Outside The Kitchen

Restaurants, eateries, and all of the *other* places where **we** can go to eat delicious meals…

My new guy and I **absolutely** LOVE going to each new place we find, or revisiting places that we both regard as 'old friends'. We constantly experiment with new places to have a meal…

Oh, and more book sales means we can do this a lot more, and then we get working on one of our many planned business ventures we want to pursue… It's a dream I have that's influenced by the various food blogs I read and the food programmes I like to watch.

The same principle introduced earlier about how you should treat your home cooking as something positive and as a replacement for bad eating habits **should** also be applied to eating out.

Cast aside the fast food or junk food places, and go instead for somewhere that serves a **healthier** option.

Some more power words for you: **Healthy DOES NOT mean boring.**

I'm a **foodie,** and I love eating nice meals…

I *love* to cook, but when I **can** go to a restaurant for a meal I **do** know what I want as "good, delicious food."

I think that enjoying a meal is part of one's well-being and that it gives us comfort and, in the case of more expensive places to eat a meal, a sense of reward. From a psychological

My new guy helped me through the tough days after becoming aware of how bad my situation was because of the situation my 'ex' had left me in, so to help me regain a sense of self-worth he'd send me money and tell me to treat myself to a meal out - adding often enough he wishes that he could be there with me…

So, how does all *this* fit into your own life?

Just you want to do with your cooked meals, where you allow yourself one food to be an indulgence, you want to treat this as your "life indulgence."

*Do make sure you CAN afford to go for these meals out you might now be planning. Even if you **can** go just once a month, or once every few months, try to include this activity into your life.*

It also means you meet people, and interaction with other people will do you a world of wonders.

If you can GO it will feel like you're indulging your mind and senses…

Are you a foodie too?

No, that's just me asking a question rather it being power words. But for me being a foodie is a "power word for the senses."

If you do decide that indulging your senses **is** going to change *how* you behave then BE a foodie.

Leaning forward, and inhaling the aromatic smell of that super-delicious meal you gave yourself permission to treat yourself to, will only ever make your sense of self-worth **better**.

Setting aside the whole indulging idea, there's another reason why "going out for meals" is so good for you. I already said that 'eating out' can give you comfort and a sense of reward.

These are **crucial** components of your well-being. **Better** well-being means your life is better.

Here are a few possible 'thought processes' you can use to kick start the whole 'eating out' journeys for yourself:

How about finding a club that does some sort of communal 'eat and meet' event…
Or you create what I want to create, which is a blogging site that reviews these restaurants or eateries…
Get in touch with old friends and meet up with them in a restaurant so you have a neutral setting rather than home…

There are **endless** possibilities for eating out as an activity. Make it your own. Use it also to eliminate some of the loneliness you feel right now from your life.

And if you cannot afford it, there's also the option of asking people to visit you and eat in…

This Page Left Intentionally Blank…
for you to write in.

Chapter Ten:

Hobbies & Pastimes

Introduction

When you start getting your life in order - that's when you finances are **all** getting sorted out (though *not* necessarily with any debts paid off - remember that I said to budget for **everything** including pastimes), with your needs all addressed, with you getting all necessary help needed to get your life back on track - that's when it's time to make your "me time" **matter**…

Everyone should have a few different hobbies or pastimes to **do**. Some of these hobbies or pastimes may cost money, while others are cost-free.

For some hobbies or pastimes, you'll need to learn new skills, while others may be easy to start to do immediately. You can do this by watching YouTube or joining a site such as Skillshare).

I have several hobbies and pastimes that keep me going whenever I'm not writing books.

One of them, if you haven't guessed it yet, is cooking. I absolutely love cooking so much that want to get a few cookbooks with my creations into print… well, yes, *one day* perhaps. Dreaming like *this* is also good for cultivating more and more creativity of ANY kind.

Another pastime that I do regularly is going to discuss in the subchapter **Online Gaming**.

Doing artworks and drawing is something else I love, and have loved since early childhood as the real "me."

I also enjoy taking photos, too; somewhat an extension of doing art, and this pastime was fostered as a direct result of enjoying art.

When you feel up to it you should choose a few hobbies and pastimes for yourself.

It's a way to keep your mind **off** the problems you might be facing after a break-up (still remember what you promised yourself at the beginning of this book - it is NOT your fault that it happened, okay!!!)

Start with **easy** hobbies that **don't** cost much.

For example, writing can be a hobby initially, and if you don't own a computer (yes, some people don't have computers at all or hardly use one at all), then a notebook and a pen for a dollar store or similar will get that going.

I suggested this in the Journaling subchapter as an activity to sort out your mind, but now I'm also suggesting you can do it as a hobby, and you can even end up writing, and who knows, I might read something YOU wrote one day.

Writing actually started as a hobby for me, and I always remind myself of the words my "literary mentor" speaks: *The more you do it the easier it gets…"*

This applies to **all** hobbies or pastimes involving a **skill**. When you do them <u>regularly</u> you get better at it, and when you get better it the skills *open* doors for you.

In the next subchapter, I'll discuss a few negative aspects of being creative you do need to be aware of before you start to do them, so you come prepared with the correct mindset for doing them…

"I Can't Draw A Straight Line."

When I was a small child I remember sitting beside the other kids in kindergarten and staring over at 'them' drawing and seriously wondering why they'd draw "their people" so wrong and so "all over the place."

I still own the drawings from back then…

If I showed you one of my earliest drawings, which was done when I was perhaps four years old, it will very clearly show a real-looking woman.

Later art teachers would remark at how **proportionately correct** she is.

She has five fingers on each hand, five toes on each foot.

In art terms, it's generally stated that you can take the height of a human head, and copy it eight times to get the right height from head to toe for a properly proportioned person.

This was what I learned years later in art lessons.

I was already doing this as a four-year-old.

And "arguing" with those "other kids" over THEIR mistakes…

Oh, and **neither** *my "real me parents" can't draw to save their lives, so it doesn't matter if all YOU are capable of doing is to draw stick persons.*

There are people out there right who have made "not being able to draw well" into a unique art form in their own right. Just remember this bit of information as you read on…

Personally, I was taught by a teacher at age eleven that art is a personal expression of creativity.

Someone may paint a canvas in the most garish yellow possible then draw a stick person in one corner, and they might call this "art".

Some people call what Banksy does "art".

Some people like a Rembrandt painting.

Someone else is more into Van Gogh.

Each person is entitled to their *own* taste in art.

Similarly, everyone can like a different book, a different style of music, different movies or television programmes…

So, what has *this* all to do with the title of this chapter? That's what you're now thinking, right?

Well, despite arguing with those kids - actually it had led to getting *two* best friends out of it for a while, so it was done as banter really - it taught me early on that art is subjective, that the skill is highly personal, and it doesn't matter if one person has this skill and the next person does not.

Remember now what I said about *my* parents who always told **me** - as I grew up - that *they* didn't know WHERE my skill came from.

Never ever…

Similarly, if I swap the drawing to singing (as an example) then you'd have a person to endure who'd be butchering every one of your favourite songs because I can't sing.

For me, singing is similar in nature to what the act of drawing of stick people to others might be.

So, if you want to embrace your creativity don't worry about being very good at it. If you can't do a sum you use a calculator. If you can't draw a straight line you'd use a ruler.

Just remember what I said *before*.

If you keep DOING an exercise of any kind over and over, and if you keep REPEATING a skill you're trying to learn or get better at, you WILL get better at it as time goes by.

Art comes in so many forms that we could probably deck out every street of London with artwork if we wanted to - okay, I'm just *guessing* here by the way.

But just as there are some hundred billion books in existence that each represents a different amount of skill and capability, there are likely as many artworks as well.

Or more…

Whatever you **do** decide to create it is **your** choice to show it off, or not.

Actually, don't be afraid to show it off, and remember that expression in art **is** personal and subjective, whichever medium it may be. There is always someone out there who will admire it, love it and appreciate that you shared it with them…

Experiment With Creativity

When I get doing other creativity, other than my writing, I like to experiment with doing creative things such as doing my artwork, but also crafting, photography, cooking or any other number of things, often things that are rather experimental in nature…

Also, because my new guy enjoys getting involved in this act of being creative we've gotten some interesting things done around the home. I started with this sort of creativity just a few months after my 'ex' had gone and I've never stopped.

Doing this stuff takes my mind off everyday life.

It's relaxing. Very, very relaxing…

Creativity starts in the mind.

As you have read I made the suggestion to nurture and soothe your mind in the first two chapters. I did this for a reason.

Here are a few things that guide my "everyday life" and how they apply to everyday life.

1) My happy mind finds it easier to be creative and find beauty in things.

2) My mind knows what it wants from life and enriches it with creativity.

3) My mind's capacity to reason and understand things is always growing.

On the blank page, at the end of this chapter, write three sentences representing positive suggestions about creativity that will help you grow your personal creative drive. Now, *how* does creativity connect with anything else I've been talking about? *Why* is it so important to pursue creativity in your life?

In **Go Creative** I suggested that you can learn new skills from being creative. In fact, I'm convinced that it keeps the mind young and active.

As an example, I'll tell you something that happened to someone I knew. She's passed away now, but before this lady passed away she would sit every day and put together puzzles. Meanwhile, she was diagnosed with Alzheimer's. But she kept going and going, and I'm convinced she held on to a good life for so much longer because she was creative with her mind...

Yes, doing puzzles **is** a form of creativity *often* overlooked. **Hand and eye** coordination are what helps a person when they're creative, and for puzzles, this is the crucial aspect of the activity. So while you may think that "being creative" isn't needed, science shows it's crucial for one's well-being...

Online Gaming

I'm a gamer. There. I admitted it. The reason I keep doing sort of this activity, and why I love it, is because it's where I met my new guy. He loves it too, and I think that some of our most relaxing time and most conversational times are when we play computer games.

Also, when we play computer games it's when my new guy and I don't take ourselves seriously in the slightest…

Yes, you can meet the new person **online** and actually be successful with long-distance dating, and even more so if you do what I suggested with the 'mind over mind.'

I have to point out immediately that both my new guy and I are in our early fifties (or I will join him past the '50 mark' a few weeks after this book is published).

We both play an online game called World of Warcraft.

This game is one of the thousands of computer games that exist, so if this game doesn't sound like your sort of game there are plenty of others to choose from.

I do want to add that the back story of this game directly influenced the real "me" into the world of storytelling, and is the direct catalyst for why I became an author.

Here's a brief outline of how my new guy and I actually met in this game.

We were both in the same 'guild.'

One day, I needed help with something in the game, and the rest is history…or *maybe* the start of one of the most unusual romance novels being written because, as you may have guessed by now (or even at the time you read the *Introduction*, we met in unusual circumstances which kind of added pressure on me as to whether I would be able to fall in love in this way.

I'm writing this book under an *assumed* name, and I do this mostly to protect against anything my 'ex' might say or do in respect of my presentation of facts.

Even though there's only about one per cent of the total text is a direct description of my 'ex'.

My 'ex' would even freak out at the idea of being mentioned in any book, unlike my new guy who feels proud of me want to open up about a painful part of my life and likes it that he's the model for the "good guy" you should be attracting to your life now you've had the inspiration for such behaviour from this book.

While as the real "me" I'm actually writing a fiction novel about my new guy and I meeting in such an unusual way.

I plan on getting this romance story finished by the end of 2019.

It's going to be a beautiful love story that will show you that second chances can happen (just check my publisher's news feed for news about when that book is published).

Perhaps, one day, I'll tell the world outright that **this** pen name belongs to **me**, and my 'ex' be damned if he tries to do anything.

I've made an author I know the custodian of the knowledge of who is behind this book, most so she can make sure that those who need to know actually understand this book is by a real person and only written under an assumed identity - a character so to speak - to protect the real "me" against anything my 'ex' might do…

Okay, enough of the doom and gloom about the 'ex'.

It's *actually* a nice thing to have something in common with my new guy **because** when we're busy playing together it also keeps bringing us closer.

You may have seen stories in the news that suggest that gaming in this way is addictive or destructive to a relationship, however, the flip side is that it doesn't need to be.

*There are literally hundreds, or even thousands, of cases where people have **met** their future spouses online, playing World of Warcraft or similar games.*

The earliest of such situations, and that they COULD even happen is from meeting a random gamer in early-2007.

*At a time this is all happening I was aware that my 'ex' was going to leave me **but** still blissfully ignorant that it WOULD happen.*

So, I met this fellow gamer, and she started telling me who "today she had one of the happiest mornings after receiving the news that her son and daughter-in-law were having their second child."

I congratulated her, and it prompted her to continue on with information of how they'd met.

Apparently, and here's where now her daughter-in-law's story and my own are similar, her daughter-in-law had broken up with her husband after two years of a very bad marriage (I have details beyond this, and also this gamer didn't know about my home situation), and apparently her son, who was in the same guild as her, had decided to help her…

He'd travelled for a hundred miles to help her pack up everything and then took her home with her.

A year later she had gotten divorced, and then another year later they married with their first child arriving six months later. That all happened about two years and bit before I met the gamer, and before got told this story…

It was in this moment that I opened up to this fellow gamer, and told her everything.

I've never forgotten her words to me: "If you are meant to be with another person he'll be there. And just like my son never thought he'd meet his future wife in this game you shouldn't forget that the best places for a future love interest to be hiding is behind an avatar in a game or any unexpected places out there…"

She was told about me meeting my new guy though she had to reveal to me that she was quitting but she did wish me well and hoped I'd found my soul mate.

If In Doubt, Join A Club

If you're **not** into the previously mentioned online dating *thing,* then joining a club might be where you meet a new love interest.

Yes, this could well be the shortest subchapter in all the book if I had a say in it but DO remember the gamer's words. She said that every person can meet someone to love and that it can be in highly unusual places. Or end up the longest because of the different anecdotal things I can conjure up from all my experiences…

For me, the "new love" happened in a computer game, and it leads to me having a long distance relationship, followed by me moving in.

It **wasn't** easy for either my new guy or myself as we were met with a lot of doubts about whether it could work.

Do you recall me saying earlier that communication **is** necessary for a relationship to work?

This is the cornerstone for anything long distance to work. Oh, and the friendship **first** as well.

Long before *any* love happened between us a strong, solid friendship was fostered between my new guy and me.

We'd talk on Skype, play World of Warcraft, and he became used to my endless chatterbox mentality.

My new guy says even TODAY that he loves listening to me just talk…talk…talk…and talk just a little bit more.

When he coaxed that chatterbox from its shy shell immediately, and because I had already started on this mission to change *how* I behaved and how my personality is, it was so much easier to do it than I ever thought possible.

He saw something in me that he explains as "a beautiful personality, smart, and a breathtaking smile to go with it." Well, this one of the many variations of the explanation.

Proof that **changing** my mindset had its benefits were shown in how my new guy saw me (and still sees me).

I guess the **best** proof I was grasping some sort of a winning formula comes from *his* current frequent suggestion/assertion that "he's in love with *his* best friend." (that best friend is ME!)

I think from the moment that he said this to me I knew I was doing something right about my process of wanting to be a difference in how I behaved and in how my personality was really.

I wanted to change even **more** because he had said this to me…

Ah, but now you're saying something like: "What has this all to do with clubs, hmm?"

Okay, here's the thing. For the last few months of my writing process whenever I took a break I would watch the news. Then in commercial breaks, I'd see this thing about something called Boxwars. Because of my own gaming background, this thing called Boxwars has some quirky appeal to me even if I wouldn't do it myself. Although that said, I *may* go watch it as an activity at some point for a **good** laugh and a fun day out with my new guy… (just need to convince him to go)

That's what I mean by "If in doubt, join a club."

It's another way you make new friends or connections. It's a place for socialising. It's where you can learn new things or experience new things. It's where you could meet someone…

It's actually rather ironic in ways, even odd, that I would discuss this as a topic seeing I had met my 'ex' in a club originally. But hind side, I do still value it as a good thing to do. However, if I was going to the same club now and not back when I met him originally, I'd be a lot more cautious about who I'd interact with.

Being **careful** is essential in ALL situations when it comes to meeting new people. But don't let it stop you from socialising and enjoying life…

This Page Left Intentionally Blank...
for you to write in.

Chapter Eleven:

Intro Going Outro

Introduction

It was in my mid-teens that I *first* knew something was *wrong* about how I felt about myself. Months later, and three counsellors later, I knew a **name** for it. I knew I had <u>clinical depression</u>.

Fast forward to around the time when I had started to date my 'ex,' and I'd been working on overcoming this condition.

I was actually 'quite successful' with coping with the depression and I was starting to overcome it, but never as well as I did after meeting my new guy. Compared to now I was rather vulnerable…

Little did I know that more than a decade *later* I'd face a harder battle of overcoming this condition when it slammed me down to the lowest point of a deep dark pit of despair, a mind pained by the hurt of words and a body unable to keep the pain hidden. I know the pain of feeling an irrational fear that cannot be explained away, where leaving the house is a chore and where being around people is impossible…

Against this downward spiral, I was coping, just marginally, with a daily battering round of mental and verbal abuse from the guy who was supposed to love me and who'd promised *me* we'd grow old together.

The latter - the possibility of growing old with someone who loves you unconditionally - is something I **DO** have now.

My new guy is someone I'm going to grow old with…

But so much of my life between 1996 (when the first hints of the abusive behaviour started to show themselves) and August 2007 (when he was finally gone) is stuff I still have going through my mind.

It's what compels me into writing this book so that others can see this sort of situation in their own live OR in that of others around them…

My 'ex' couldn't *even* let things be somewhat "okay" for me *after* telling me he was leaving. He *had* to add to this six months of additional destructive behaviour.

Not every "break-up" is amicable, even though I **do** know of people who split up amicably, or without the two people in the relationship tearing one another apart.

The **above** is the darker version that *some* of those reading this book **may** recognise in their own life right now - both the aspects of life growing up with this condition as well as recognising the feelings that may exist as a direct consequence of the treatment received.

The other sort of break-up, that of just being abandoned isn't nice either.

Only a short time before completing this book I heard of one such sort of break-up, and it involves a kind soul who does YouTube and in this version of a break-up it didn't just cause a break-up, but also she lost half of what gave her life as a YouTuber meaning.

In a way, her situation did also touch me because what's worse than first going through the wringer and then be abandoned on top of it all.

My story of recovery isn't over yet. I was told that recovering from what my 'ex' did to me may take a decade or longer. But I have my new guy to spur me on to live for better things.

One of those many things is to become a more extrovert sort of person, for me not to keep being afraid any more, and to TELL my story through a medium I discovered: **writing**.

Dealing With Anxiety

I imagine you're sitting on your sofa *or* your bed right now. I imagine that, in this moment of time, you feel like the *whole* world is spinning around you, and the thought of **going outside** makes you physically sick. You'd get you into panic mode as you're supposed to go somewhere important...

Yes, I know the feeling **very** well. You have read my description in the previous subchapter, so you have some insight into my mindset of back then.

Dealing with those events on a daily basis is what lead me to have anxiety as a condition to deal with as well - I also had to deal with depression.

It was much later, a month or so after my 'ex' had gone from my life when I saw a doctor who finally was able to explain that everything I'd experienced was post-traumatic stress disorder (PTSD).

This condition is often known as the condition that soldiers who've been in war arrive home with.

Or, at least, that's where I knew it from…

Studying this condition has led me to realise that there are *many* reasons for it to occur in a person's life, and not just by being on a war front.

Other events that can contribute to it to occur include sexual assault, such as a brutal rape, a bad traffic collision or other similar events, child abuse, or perhaps such an event such as being caught up in an earthquake or other natural disasters can cause it *too* I'd guess.

But *not* every person develops this condition.

I'm guessing that one's natural coping mechanisms **play** a role in whether you cope, or not.

It *has* been identified to contribute to a person having a higher risk of suicide or self-harm.

Anxiety may be mild compared to this condition, but it can be as debilitating and it can also have an adverse consequence as to how a person lives their life.

My anxiety started to affect me after some events which I'm **not** going to describe here as my 'ex' would recognise the details of it, and I don't want to include too much of such stuff in this book.

I **will** tell you it was of a sexual nature and when I went for counselling after my 'ex' had left the counsellor decided to identify it as rape or sexual assault.

The *events* in question left me feeling fearful of being around my 'ex,' and according to the counsellor I'd developed my PTSD because I had been dealing with the event without any safety net to pull me back from the "abyss."

She said that it was *likely* I'd dealt with anxiety for five years or more by the time I saw her and that I'd dealt with the PTSD for the previous two years (since the events happened at least).

But despite the mind-numbing pain caused by these two conditions, as well as daily life of depression, the counsellor remarked I had unusual **inner strength**.

Proof that I *could* help people with this **inner strength**, and which is an event that ultimately leads to **me** wanting to do this book, is something that happened a few months after the counselling had finally ended (the reason for ending it was the fact I had met my new guy).

I remember someone telling me "You are stronger than you think you are," and this had been something I'd been telling myself for a long time already at the time - so in a way, the process of forming a new mindset started earlier than a decade ago perhaps.

The name of this book is "Heartbreak Doesn't Last Forever." There's actually a back story to WHY it has *this* name…

While walking in the town I was surprised when I was stopped from walking on by a woman.

After a few minutes of speaking to me, I realised *who* she is. I remembered then a woman sitting as I left one of the first counselling session. The woman talking to me said then that she needed to thank me.

I was curious what for…

She said **this** to me:

"I know because of what I heard you say that my heartbreak won't last and it is what I heard you say to the counsellor is why I'm now safe and away from my abusive ex-husband…"

She wasn't alone in the street. I think the man with her was her father.

When I decided to write this book I remembered HER words to the real "me" and decided to call the book a name that reflected the words she said. She said, "heartbreak won't last."

What she told me that breezy morning is that my heartbreak wouldn't last EITHER.

That's the moment when I stopped feeling so anxious.

That's when *my* healing started…

Talking As Therapy: Be Your Own Therapist!

Okay, so from the get-go this isn't a substitute for actually getting proper therapy from someone specialising in the field of marriage counselling or counselling to deal with depression or anxiety, or any other counselling that you may need or want to get…

I'm going to say **immediately** that counselling is **very** good for *every* person who <u>needs</u> it.

If you feel uncomfortable about going to one, consider talking to the pastor or priest of your church instead. Or check for specialist help groups where you can just get to talk in a group about what's on your mind.

Whichever option you *go* with, talking to someone **neutral** who isn't directly linked *or* involved with your home life.

My own story with dealing with counsellors has a huge contrast in the negative and the positive because one of the *first* counsellors I ever met was so *negative* about the idea of a teenager coping with depression.

I saw him maybe *six* times before I quit going. He'd said that "only older people can get depressed" which was one of the most stupid things I had heard back then, and even now I think it's stupid…

But it hammers home that you need to get along with the person you'll see every week for a number of months or as much as a few years (the time it takes for you to get better depends on how affected by the cause of it you were).

I suggest going to a counsellor few at least three months. However, you CAN ask them for suggestions of how to make stuff easier. I use power words in this book because MY counsellor used them and said that they're good for motivating the mind into a different mindset (and that's also where my whole idea of "nurture the mind, soothe the mind" evolved from.

*Mind you, I'd say that for someone, who is a Christian, the words from the Bible - if used properly and **not** used for negative ideas - can be power words too…*

If you find yourself a counsellor the first conversation with them needs to establish whether they are a good match for you. Because it's so simple. Your healing starts from having trust in the person helping you and trust here is gained in the same way as with new friendships, new work colleagues and ultimately the new guy or girl in your life for a new relationship. You'll have a professional relationship with the counsellor, and getting along with them helps you in the long run…

Where you come in as your own therapist, is why I suggested first of all to change your mindset in the first two chapters.

Okay, I'll come clean. I've been coaxing you into a mindset which isn't only relying on others to fix stuff for you, but instead, you're evolving a mindset where you help yourself in every way possible.

Now either you'll slam this book shut right now because here you thought you were just reading someone's story about life after a break-up and/or divorce and now she's telling you that you have to work on this stuff…

(The latter may turn into a few not-so-glorious reviews on Amazon, but I DO hope that statistically, I'm going to have a runaway train with this book…I guess that's my 2019 daydream sorted out now).

Maybe you're laughing uncontrollably at **my** ability to be humorous in the most inappropriate way possible.

Laughing at MY **stupid** mind that thinks it's always giving **me** a leg-up in comparison to what the "experts" tell me. Yes, that's how far I went with all this self-help, and being my own therapist.

Now, *why* would I know better than them?

It's simple. NO, I'm not an expert.

However, I **know** my mind better than they do. I **know** how I feel better than they do. I **know** my past and they don't. All *they* get is small fragments of all this of what I might feel comfortable to share with even the nicest counsellor or therapist, so their help is always going to be <u>incomplete</u> IF that's the only thing I rely on or IF you rely on it.

This is why this book is about how I did stuff and packed with suggestions of how you can adapt to your own situation.

Hence why I suggest to annotate endlessly, make notes in the margins, use a highlighter to mark sentences that work for you or speak to you, and to make notes on every blank space you can find.

(I'm expecting the photos of the book done in such a way too by the way at nleeauthor@gmail.com).

But if you're still reading instead, this is the thing I discovered as the years went by, first from doing what the experts tell me, then reading books as often as I can, and now by analysing the past and figuring out how I can help others with the wisdom I gained. I may not be an expert by I think that sharing stories such as what I went through is what will help others cope with dealing with their own situations, and I'm a believer in paying it forward so that's **why** I wrote this book.

Learning To Cope With The Aftermath

And now for the encore, the aftermath, the end that starts a new beginning…

It doesn't matter *what* you call it. And so begins a little story. This is an **actual** situation I'm dealing with ever since I had a "blast from the past" so to speak.

First of all remember the following: There **will** be a time when the pain lessens when you need to move on, put the past behind you and stop dwelling on past events…as I was reminded about so unexpectedly while still working on this book.

I was reminded of what it means to try to put blame on someone else for mistakes made when I got an email from someone. My reaction to it made me realise how changed I am.

Even if I'm not going to say what the situation is. It's a situation that reminds me again how necessary it is to always put me first.

Yes, some of you may assume this is rather selfish of me but the sender of the email is one of the people who caused me to have to work on changing myself in the first place.

*The **bad** part of how they wrote their email is that they refuse to take the blame for their own behaviour which had caused me to hurt…*

I'd say that three or four years ago I **wouldn't** have reacted in the way I did when I saw the email.

I wasn't angry, sad, annoyed when I read the email. I reacted with a neutrality that surprised **me**.

When I told my new guy about the email I explained so 'matter of fact' that **he** was probably surprised about **me**.

When I mentioned about the "blaming" in this book I always thought some of those who know the real "me" wouldn't be the same as when I had contact with them, but this incident shows me how wrong I can be at times.

This person STILL assumes blame is with *others*, and not with themselves.

YET a small part of the email also shows the individual from that email, had actually started to realise **they** had done *wrongs…*

I think the email made me realise how **tough** it can be for people to realise in what way they were or are behaving.

It also shows, to a degree, the reasoning I have myself that for a person to move past the pain of a break-up he or she has to set aside the idea of blaming the other person.

Which is **one** reason I have pity for my 'ex' rather than blaming him, and that's how I cope so much better now with life, in general, these days…

But that said, the message from this person DID put things in perspective for me.

Because, in a way, I recognised some of the SAME processes I'd gone through in the way they worded their 'regret.'

But despite the regret, this individual had not realised yet that they couldn't blame the other person - that being ME - for whatever had happened to them.

They **know** what I had said before I severed contact with them (the reasons for it won't be elaborated here), and now I see someone who is ME of a decade ago.

So, the aftermath of a break-up or the loss of a friendship with the individual in question is an ongoing situation rather than something you can give an end-date for.

How **you** cope with it depends on *how* you grow as a person.

But if you're like me, and find yourself standing at an impasse similar to what's reflected in this following sentence: "do I move on from this when the "past" comes knocking on your door?" - which, as you know from reading the book did happen when my 'ex' turned up one day - so, do I also let this person into my life again…or *not*.

How I'm going to cope with the aftermath of that particular situation (which is what the email was about) is going to be addressed if this person does contact me again.

How I *will* cope with contact with this person…?

I guess I'll have to write a follow-on book to let you *know*.

I'll leave you with a cliffhanger here….

(How dare N. Lee to leave me now with a cliffhanger about another life lesson in a non-fiction memoir about her life after divorce…huh…???)

Blossoming Bloom

When you find that **happy self** again, declare yourself a **blossoming bloom**. Have you *ever* looked at flowers just after a pour down of spring rain?

Flowers have this tendency to open *just* at the right moment when the rain has almost stopped or completely stopped.

It's in **that** moment nature for me possesses the greatest beauty.

I like to compare the things that have happened in my life to nature. Most notably to nature's ability for renewal...

For example, it sounds *so* much better to be like a caterpillar going into a cocoon and then becomes a butterfly.

In a way, that butterfly is **me**...after I've sorted out just a *bit* more of my life, and made it just a fraction more at its best, and am a little happier with myself (as I said before depression is something that doesn't go away easily).

I'm fully aware that life has its many ups and downs. You should be aware of it too.

Remember the *wheel* I mentioned earlier.

If you didn't buy into that idea, maybe the idea of a butterfly is a bit better. It's definitely prettier than some old boring wheel.

But **either** option is what is the driving force behind what I want to discuss here.

I realised fast, within a year or two that in order to find a new person to make me happy I had to be happy first, and I had to make sure that I had changed, and I had to force myself into a more positive outlook on life.

So look at it as shown in the following illustration…

Before you bought this book you were the caterpillar.

While **reading** this book (it doesn't matter if you do it in one sitting or you tackle a chapter every month - in fact, with 72 subchapters, you can give yourself five days to read the subchapter, do the suggested "exercises" and have time left to work on your own memoir to add to the premise of "paying it forward - YOUR story matters TOO!).

After reading this *book* you may have found your own **butterfly moment**, and thus you are the blossoming bloom I described before.

Go draw your butterfly on the blank page that follows. Just draw it the way you want it to look rather than some sort of perfect artwork, and by doing so get in touch with your creativity.

I guess you **see** a pattern in this book now. The real "me" writes fiction, and in fiction, there's a beginning, middle and end - caterpillar, cocoon, butterfly…or seed, plant, flower (and fruit occasionally). But just like a story, I wanted to add some sort of structure to this non-fiction memoir.

The **first** two chapters are the beginning of your story. They *end* with your brain rewired, your thinking <u>reshaped</u>. The **last** two chapters are the *end* of your story (at least <u>for now</u>) and **yes**, the **cliffhanger bit** is somewhat cliche *but* appropriate as you don't know what the *next* part of the story is. Everything in between is the middle part of the story and from fiction, you know this is where character grows the most.

Your life is a story and just like you don't know where the story in a book will take you, you can never know where the story of your life will go.

Just like you don't want to read about a two-dimensional character you shouldn't make yourself into a two-dimensional person. A book with well-rounded characters in it are fun to read, so make yourself into an AMAZING person with so many aspects to her or his personality that you bring the future love interest to yourself like a moth to a flame.

It was something that shone like the brightest star in my personality, as the real "me," that my new guy noticed… **remember that**.

Now **go** be that blossoming bloom…

This Page Left Intentionally Blank…
for you to write in.

Chapter Twelve:

Find Your Heart

Introduction

When you've had heartbreak it's really **hard** to find your heart again. You've heard of the expression "to wear one's heart on one's sleeve," which generally means to show your feelings and emotions freely and openly.

This approach to life *can* be tough when you've been hurt by any person (something that's happened to me *more* times I would want to dwell on), and the biggest of this sort of *hurt* comes from someone you had loved, trusted and respected for a period of time.

Throw **all** the advice out of the window and start living **first** of all for yourself.

You *will* hear things such as: *"You'll meet someone new"* or *"It will get better"* or *"You'll get over it"* as well as **harsher** things like: *"Why cry over spilt beans"* or *"He didn't do anything wrong really, not really"* or the **worst** one *"It's all your own fault anyway…"*

Now cut a piece of paper that will fit over the above wording (call it "dramatic annotation"…okay?) and fasten it over the words with some cello-tape and write in big letters on the paper the following:

"It's not my fault and I can decide how I'll find my heart again all by myself."

Now…**stop** believing these words whenever someone EVER wants to say ANY words similar to those you read *above*.

Now you want to tape these words over and never reflect on such negative thoughts ever again.

*These words **don't** exist in my own thinking patterns (except to write them here for you to reject from your life too) so they SHOULD NOT exist in yours either.*

Also, I'm convinced that we go through something akin to mourning when we end a relationship we'd invested our hearts towards. It's a painful process to let go, but eventually, we have to do this.

You **cannot** let *this* pain consume you forever, or else you won't have any room for the possible **new** love to enter in its place.

There was a time when I let this pain consume me, but these days I just reflect on what happened and always remember that tomorrow brings a better day.

In the first chapters, I suggested changing your mindset. This whole chapter is about your life once you start being ready to move on to a new existence.

By working on your mindset you change negative thoughts into more positive ones.

I'll be discussing in the rest of this chapter what to do if you do find yourself alone and cannot find someone new to be with - **it's OKAY to be alone!**

I'll tell you how you might want to deal with the two conflicting versions of your mind and personality you're dealing with right now.

And what to do to remember that you **only** need to change **yourself for yourself**, and how to prepare for that day when the new guy (or gal) does turn up in your life…

Alone Time

When you're alone you **can** actually be *so* alone that it causes you pain. Not physical pain though. It causes a deep emotional pain that takes time to go away *and* that takes time to stop affecting the mind as much as it wants to do...

However, the flip side of this happening is the 'alone time' you **choose** for yourself, and this different type of alone time *can* make you serenely contented.

There's a *stark* contrast between these polar **opposites**, and personally, I've felt *both* versions of wanting to be alone.

First of all, I'm discussing the more *negative* of these two versions of alone time in this chapter, and that's the one tied also to the aforementioned anxiety, and how it affects me personally. This is the one part of all the stuff I set out to change that I'm still working on, and I think it's the toughest part because it's the closest to the core of WHAT the conditions, depression and anxiety, do to your mind and body when you are affected by them.

This type of 'alone' is caused, at least *when* I experience it, and I still do because of the depression, by a sense of wanting to get *away* from the world.

I tend to switch off from social media as the real "me" when the feelings overwhelm me.

And, even though, the feeling is negative I've learned to use this time for more positive things such as self-reflection and in recent years also the book writing that I like to do.

The thing I've always thought *when* I reflect on this part of my life and on how I behave in this way (and it's a behaviour you cannot really escape when you are depressed or anxious) is how isolating it is in general, and mostly because I don't want to talk to anyone about **how I feel**.

In a way, I think it's these conditions that cause this sort of feeling of being alone (though not necessarily able to be referred to as loneliness) to happen.

In a way, there's loneliness attached to this life that's very self-imposing in nature.

There's a difference between wanting to be alone and loneliness.

The best way I can describe loneliness is to evoke a feeling of empathy in you…

Imagine the following scene as you read it…

You walk alone a street somewhere. It can be in your hometown or city, or a place you're visiting for a vacation.

As you glance into a side street you see a dog curled up on a piece of cardboard; you hear him whimpering softly. You look around to see if there's anyone near. You see no one.

You walk towards the dog and lean forward stretching out your hand to let the dog sniff it but the dog backs away and starts to shake uncontrollably. It's obvious to you the dog is fearful of you, though you see no reason why.

You walk off, but glancing back you see the dog looking at you with glazed eyes that tell volumes of who he feels. He's lonely and despite being afraid he wants you to stay…

If I made you get a lump in your throat and your eyes are stinging now then you understand loneliness. *This* scene is actually based on a real event.

Had I been capable of taking that dog home I would have done so. But with barely the funding to manage my bills I had to walk away, however, I spotted a policewoman, told her about the dog, and she said she'd make sure the dog was okay.

I went to see the dog from the alleyway a few times in the dog pound where he ended up at (the policewoman gave me the address) until the call came to let me know he'd been adopted.

In some ways, I *wish* I had been capable of taking in the dog because that way I wouldn't have been alone any more. I felt compassion for this dog because I had previously owned a rescued dog. In fact, the real "me" might end up with a newly rescued dog one day, but only if my new guy and I can afford it (hmm, those book sales would help in that).

But in **another** way the dog *did* help me because he forced me to leave the house and go outside, and oh boy, that was so difficult with the anxiety holding me in its grip…

Being alone though, differently from being lonely, is perfectly okay. 'Being alone' simply means you want time alone for whatever you're doing, though I do make a distinction between "me time" and "alone time."

"Me time" is where you have people around you and you make time to be away from contact with them.

"Alone time" is where you are alone, and choose to stay alone by not seeking out having people near you.

These are MY explanations of these words, and other people are entitled to their own way of explaining these words.

I like to create my **own** interpretation of stuff I learn, though I always still pay attention to the advice the original offered.

It can be possible to stand in the middle of a massive crowd of people, to glance around and to feel deep loneliness. After all, humans are in general a social being. But despite this, it can also feel as good to just be alone as the individual matters just as much.

As Spock would say: "Logic clearly dictates that the needs of the many outweigh the needs of the few."

But do they?

Not necessarily… yes, that was my answer in my mind when I heard this sentence for the first time while watching the movie. However, Spock, as played by the late Leonard Nimoy, as an individual **did** *also become the character I identify the most with ever since because to me the character represents closest who I am as an individual as the real "me." I'm unique yet part of a bigger crowd. I'm alone yet not necessarily lonely. I'm lonely but never alone… (yes, this is the mindset of the teenager that decided to be philosophical about a science fiction movie).*

Me vs You

No, this **isn't** a suggestion of 'N. Lee' versus 'whoever is the reader of this book' - although I **do** hope that *many* people will be reading this book, and they're getting something valuable from it.

The "me," in this context, is your world seen by *you*, and the "you" is when you look in the nearest mirror and stare at the reflection staring back at you.

It refers to the possible viewpoint that your world is based around the idea that you're always going to see the worst in yourself, and that you'll always be telling yourself that your not the worst person out there.

I think **most** humans struggle with this idea of being the *worst* person in some way…

In the book writing world, I've heard a phrase to describe this in a more tangent way, and people talking about it refer to it as "impostor syndrome."

But it's not an idea invented there or unique to writers…

Every creative person feels like they're an "impostor" at some point during their career.

Also, every person in a job or running a business feels this way. It can crop up when business isn't going so well.

Politicians may feel this way too, even they don't tend to show it publicly. Or if they do they brush off the questions about their behaviour.

Students in a top university might feel this way during exam time, and it can possibly get in the way of them doing well during the stressful times of such exams.

A person who is bullied in school feels it too, and in their case, the impostor syndrome may take on the version of feeling less entitled to friendship than others.

Within relationships, the impostor syndrome takes hold in the form of one person in the relationship feeling less important, less in control, or less of a person compared to the other.

In fact, as it seems, according to "some" advice being spread by "some" people on YouTube, that relationships should *only ever* be about bullying or dominance by one individual in a relationship towards the other, IF you were to accept what those people are claiming as a *truth* somehow…

I'm not going to reveal the sources of the following STUPID suggestions so not to get sued, but these are OTHER people's suggestions and not reflective of my own ideas. I'm including them to illustrate what sort of stupidity exists out there in the wider world.

Just don't listen to such notions and you'll be better of…

They may suggest that somehow a man is 'supposedly' superior to a woman. They are equals…

Another **ridiculous** idea spread around is that a relationship between two gays or two lesbians isn't real…

Remember that I stated that this book is for **everyone**, *and I'd go as far as to say that other than it is about the aftermath of my own break-up with my 'ex,' and about me meeting my new guy this entire book is a GENDER NEUTRAL publication.*

So swap things appropriately if you're in a different type of relationship…

…Or that a man can be horrible to a woman because she's *somehow* not as good as he is (and the YouTube persons who claim this never seem to be able to how or why without sounding like utter idiots…

ALL of this is ideas that, according to the real "me," are stupid, ridiculous, and that everyone should stop believing in or agreeing to…

I'll tell you from the get-go that my new guy disagrees with the notion of inequality in our relationship and that, according to him, we both matter.

Someone, who thinks that **he** or **she** has this impostor syndrome - often people don't realise they think of themselves in this way until they're told what this impostor syndrome is - will think that *they* are the *lesser* in a relationship.

Yes, it's generally this idea that causes the "bully" in the relationship to be a bully.

It's that behaviour BY THAT PERSON which caused your break-up, and NOT ANY of your behaviour. OKAY????

Also, remember that I told you you're NOT a victim. OKAY????

The **inner battle** of taking control of your life after a break-up is this "me vs you" as well.

You're going to be battling with the idea that *somehow* your life has come to an end.

And that you're just as you were described by your ex - may this be the ex-boyfriend, ex-girlfriend, ex-husband, ex-wife, ex-friend, or that family member you've had a falling out with…

This is the sort of conflict I have previously stated that personally, I don't like so much.

Conflict **does** happen when there's any sort of break-up, even if it seems "amicable" on the surface.

Like that ripple effect caused by a stone thrown into a still pond, you don't know what the effects are of a break-up. You cannot see the "effect" of the "cause" under the surface.

The inner battle you feel raging inside you, where you try to justify the BAD behaviour done towards you with a response such as "but he loves me" is what you need to overcome.

Psst, let me tell you a secret…

I deplore books where the sort of behaviour I describe here is somehow "glorified."

Stories which suggest that the "bad boy" doing his abusive behaviour (whether it may be verbally, emotionally, mentally, physically or sexually) are books YOU need to avoid reading.

They will just reinforce the idea that somehow you were treated in a way that was okay when it was NOT OKAY.

Instead, go for books that have these "happily ever after" themes to them because, in a way, they will also reinforce something that changes your mindset.

I wish authors stopped with the "glorified bullying in relationships" really… the real "me" wishes that…

*(Okay, some people **may** enjoy these sort of books BUT in the context of conflict I think it's better to read other types of books to help your mindset and to help your general mood).*

Remember also that if you have been bullied, whether if it is in school, college, university, work or a relationship with a person who is supposed to love you, you do yourself a world of good by seeking out counselling for the effects on you from the bullying. Bullying does leave invisible scars in your emotions, habits and behaviour that a specialist counsellor can recognise (the counsellor I saw recognised my inner scars by the way).

FIND THE HELP AS SOON AS YOU CAN, the sooner is better and you have to judge for yourself what sort of help is best for you.

The above may be the only bit of proper "self-help advice" I've put in this book but the welfare of the readers of this book matters to me.

If you're at risk in your relationship ALWAYS seek help; from the police if needed…

Now you have also a clue what I meant by *"Yes, welcome to the mindset of a person who decided to be so different that she ended up 'scaring' the 'ex' when he did decide to pay a visit"* in the subchapter **Take Action For Better Things**.

Oh, and without a doubt…my 'ex' was **always** a bully, and the real "me" had ONLY started to realise this **fact** AFTER he'd gone…

Change What?

"So, now what?" you are now asking in the penultimate subchapter of this book. "Do I end up without this heartbreak, or what?"

The answer is: *"Yes, but you need to work at it."*

My own pain, caused by heartbreak lessened in the first months after meeting my new guy, and then it went away ever so slowly. Now, it's replaced by the joy of this life I have with him around me…

I don't know *how* my life would have been like if I'd never met my new guy. I **don't** even want to dwell on that thought.

To me the idea of this is too much of this "What if…" and to me it feels like I'm going back to an earlier "What if…" involving the first thought in September 2017 when I thought: "What if things were different we never split?" or even worse: "What if I just went along with how he wants things?"

I realised **soon** thereafter that neither was an option because both options wouldn't give me the outcome I, instead, got from the years of changing my mindset, changing my behaviour, making myself healthier or making myself realise that I should put myself FIRST.

The moment you know that you come FIRST, that's when the answer to the question I started with comes to the forefront.

You **will be** in a better place, and you're in the driving seat to make it happen. I promise you that this thought will become easier as time goes by.

Also, remember that "single life" is not something to feel regrets over. If you don't meet the right person to share a life with then you should just keep loving yourself first.

YOU ALWAYS COME FIRST!!! (the most powerful power words in this book, and in my opinion this idea is in no way selfish even if people might try to convince you of it otherwise).

Believing in something is a key to this. Let's make YOU that something.

You <u>may</u> have read this book (so far!) in one sitting (or a few), and just gone through it all in a day or two.

But DO remember what I told you about my own life and my own process of change. I didn't do it in a day, a week or a month.

Or even a year, which this book suggests as a timeline for the process to begin.

I had almost **eleven** years to change myself. I do my changing even *now* as I write my book.

For the real "me" life from 2019 onward and beyond will be different. My new guy and I will be married during that year, I'll be writing who knows which book on my long list of books, doing more art as the year progresses, and taking photos to use in both art and book covers, making crafted things, working on getting "the business" going with my new guy.

The change to make this "new version" of me started in 2007, but it doesn't ever end or complete itself as a process (who knows, perhaps a follow-on book to this one with more of my "wisdom" in it?).

I regard life as a lifelong process of learning.

The biggest lesson to learn: being a better person than you were before. I hope this book gives a tiny insight into why this biggest lesson is still ongoing.

Yes, me and my oh so messy mind…right?

If you *did* get something positive from *this* book it would so COOL if I'd receive a letter about it from **you** at nleeauthor@gmail.com.

Tell me **HOW** I changed you; **what** from this book helped you. I **want** to write more "N. Lee Books" about all sorts of different topics that would **help** a person in one way or another. If you **want** to keep in touch you can send suggestions to the above-listed email address.

I won't be able to respond to emails due to time constraints and for privacy reasons. Your email address will NOT be added to any mailing list. I respect the GDPR regulations and the details of my publisher are in the front of this book, and you can search them out on Facebook. If you do want updates, you simply Like their Facebook page and they'll publish updates about new books from 'N. Lee".

Anyway, enough of this self-promoting. Though, that's how you should BE yourself with the NEW YOU that you, hopefully, have become because of reading this book. The new you should put this new self on public display.

I believe in you and I know that there was at least one chapter in this book that helped you and if there was then tell me what in this book ended up helping… okay?

The New Guy or Girl in your LIFE!

When the day comes, and you do find yourself with a new guy (or girl) in your life, that's the day when you need to set *aside* what happened **before** *if* what came before was a **bad** relationship.

Never ever bring it into a new relationship as luggage.

Yes, you <u>can</u> discuss things with the new guy (or girl) **but** you shouldn't put **any** expectations on them in terms of how to act around you, how to treat you *or* how to love you…

At the beginning of this book, I said I still call my new guy this way so to distinguish between my 'ex' and the person I'm with now.

Whenever I discuss things with my new guy, and I tell him about something I had experienced in my old life I never say: *"Such and such you're doing right now is what my ex-husband would do, and…"*

In fact, I'd go as far as saying that it's almost like oranges and apples when we talk in terms of how my new guy is compared to how my 'ex' was.

"The orange (the new guy) is doing way better than the apple (ex) in terms of being a good listener…"

We (my new guy and I) discuss a topic, and often it has **no** relation to whatever it is that we're doing at that moment. We've found that cooking time is perfect to talk about stuff.

You cannot talk about it in an endless stream, even when my current guy does say he loves listening to me talking and doesn't mind a half-hour monologue from me.

But, talking about the past isn't when I want to do such things.

I rather talk about **hopes and dreams** with my new guy. Yes, we do a remarkable amount of daydreaming but that's also the glue that keeps a relationship grounded in my opinion.

So, while cooking the discussions are chopped up into small parts, and often I will even find myself just talking about half the stuff, or one or two things, instead of everything.

The mind can decide when it's appropriate to talk, and for how long or how much or what the topic should BE.

So, when you have met that new person you want to take on a forward-looking stance for your own benefit, and subsequently theirs too.

Then you want to work on 'binding your soul with theirs,' for your hearts to find common ground, for each to become content in each of your new roles as part of a 'couple.'

Get out a notepad rather than doing this on the last pages of this book (I may sort out a dedicated companion workbook for this book if at any time there are enough requests for it) and I would like you to write a few small essays:

- On the first page, you should write a letter to your heart, telling it what way you feel right now.

- On the second page, you should write a letter to your new guy or girl, asking in it what made interested in you. If you're not with anyone right now imagine in your mind what sort of person you would like to be with.

- On the third page, you should write a letter in which you forgive your past life and thank it for the good parts.

- On the fourth (and final) page, you should list four (or more) things you hope to gain from the new relationship.

There's no right or wrong way of how these letters end up in their content, and they're meant as a final inward reflection of how you feel now you've allowed your heart to heal somewhat.

Now write on the last two pages the things you want to happen because you allowed your mindset to change.

Also, remember that it still takes more time for the heartbreak to be healed. Add one final thing to your list on the fourth page right now in your own handwriting. Write there that heartbreak doesn't last forever.

Seeing affirmative words in your handwriting often has a lot more power to heal and to affirm better than they might do as printed words.

Now, also remember that you can go through the processes talked about in this book as often as you want, and you don't ever need to do them in the same order.

Whether you read this book in a few days, weeks or months (or longer), repeating a process to heal oneself is **also** a way to recommit the process of recovering from a breakup back into your mind.

You're at the steering wheel.

You guide the process of recovery in the long run.

You decide how much time is needed.

But if you **do** want the new person in your life, this is also what you control?

You control **who** you end up with, what personality traits you look for in such a person, and ultimately you have the power in your own hands to learn to trust again.

You may want to count in this book right now how often I actually talked about my ex-husband despite over the course of this book. This book was a memoir about my feelings, my learning processes and for me to show you what I did to get a new self.

I opened this chapter with the *typical* trope about **not** bringing an old relationship into a new one, however, there's no rule that says you cannot share your worries and insecurities with a new guy or girl.

They **would** know pretty fast that you were in another relationship.

And *then* their questions might start...

Talking about so-called tropes, there's that typical one called the "blame game". Early in this book, I said to take on the stance that a breakup is not your fault…or theirs. No none of this blame game.

No blaming yourself.

No blaming them.

That's what brings doubt into the picture. Hence why I said in Put The Past In The Past that you *can* reflect on it but **not** apply it.

So, *my* advice to **you**, now you've read through this book for hours, days or weeks (I hope!) is to go **enjoy** your life with the new guy or girl you will meet. Set your goals, dreams and aspirations **together**.

Never ever forget that communication is the DNA that binds your relationship, and saying this makes this book immediately also useful for that person looking for their first love.

Life is all about relationships of **any kind**.

Whether it's a friend or best friend at school, the person you share that first kiss with, the person you married and who then gave you that heartbreak you feel right now, or the person you're with and whom you know to be the person you grow old with **and** who is healing this heartbreak their love for you.

Even with a solid friendship or love the relationship changes, evolved, has its ups and downs.

YOU and THE OTHER PERSON are the two people who make it happen.

Heartbreak won't last forever, even if you are alone for the remainder of your life. Those who can help you heal are family members (including any children you may have), friends, and people you encounter through social media. Common causes bind people **too** by the way…

If a relationship is DNA, then **love** is the lifeblood. Love comes in **many** forms. Even the kind person holding a door open for you **is** a form of love. Your appreciative smile back **is** love. A person saying "Thank You" is a form of love…

Heartbreak can only last as long as you keep the love outside.

Let it in whatever way it wants to come in.

You cannot keep the 'heart' broken if you start to live again…

Welcome to the FIRST day of the REST of your life!

Also, remember this…. YOU MATTER!!!

This Page Left Intentionally Blank...
for you to write in.

This Page Left Intentionally Blank...
for you to write in.

(for things you want to write down as your daydreams)